A Message from the Throne Room

A Message from the Throne Room

ANITA LAHANMI

To order additional copies of this book, contact:
Xlibris Corporation
0-800-644-6988
www.XlibrisPublishing.co.uk
Orders@XlibrisPublishing.co.uk
302148

Contents

Dedication   ix

Acknowledgements   xi

Foreword   xiii

Introduction   1

This Thing Called Faith . . .   3

Against All Odds!   4

God's Word—The Final Say   6

Faith Is . . .   8

Have Faith in God   10

Seeing Isn't Believing   12

Another Look at Abraham   14

When You Need Healing . . .   16

A Touch Is All You Need   17

What Do You Want from Him?   19

He Is Your Healer!   21

Courage in the Face of Fear . . .   23

Be Bold and Courageous   24

Do It Afraid   26

Ding-Dong, Goliath Is Dead!   28

Walking on Water   30

Where Do You Stand?   32

Searching for Purpose . . .   34

Do You Have a Dream?   35

Created to Succeed   37

You Are the Solution   39

Show Me the Way!   41

What Have You Done for Others Lately?   43

The Plan Still Stands!   45

When Struggling with Low Self-Esteem . . .   47

Intricately Woven, Fearfully Made!   48

The Potter's Touch   50

The Choice Is Yours, Choose Wisely!   52

When You Need Direction . . .   54

If You Only Knew   55

Your Will Be Done   57

Father Knows Best!   59

Speak Life   61

In Times of Need . . .   63

The Lord Is Your Shepherd   64

You Are in Safe Hands   66

Don't Worry, It's All Taken Care Of   68

Waiting on God . . .   70

When Lord, When?   71

Why Wait?   73

There Is Power in His Word   75

Battling with Insecurities . . .   77

Thank God for Weaknesses   78

Precious Treasures in Earthen Vessels   80

Consider the Ants   82

Made in His Image   84

Staying Anchored During Life's Storms ...   86
   Holding On!   87
   The Battle Is Not Yours!   89
   You Shall Not Be Moved!   91
   The Testing of Your Faith   93
   God's Armour   95

When You're Feeling Discouraged ...   97
   Just Keep Standing!   98
   The Seasons of Life   100
   You Are Not Alone   102
   Not Easily Broken   104
   He Is Your Rock   106

The Sovereignty of God ...   108
   Who Is Like God?   109
   God of Heaven and Earth   111
   God Is Still God!   113
   What Do You Know?   115

Glossary   119
Endnotes   121

Dedication

I dedicate this book to my loving family. We have been through so much but I know we have come out strong. We are not defeated!

To my brother Chuks, the baby of the family but a baby no more! Where did the time go? When did you stop being the little boy I took to football practice and become the man that you are today? I am so proud of you. Your determination to make something of your life despite setbacks is to be admired and praised! You have so much within you; a deep thinker with so much intelligence and the potential to accomplish great things. I pray that you will learn to lean on God and enjoy life more, for there is much to be joyful about.

To my brother Chidi, the middle child and the one my mother says never gave her any trouble in the womb. Whatever! Warm, funny and kind, you make friends easily and have the ability to draw people in. I have watched you grow from the playful, younger brother into a man of responsibility and direction. Your gentle spirit and ease with which you overlook an offense are the wonderful qualities that make you who you are. My prayer for you is that you discover and fulfil the purpose for which you were created.

To my father, my dear, dear father, Dr Louis Amaefuna. With a Doctorate in Philosophy, I'm certain that my studious nature and desire to excel in whatever I do, is a gift I have inherited from you. Although you are the quiet one in the family, there is no doubt in my mind that part of my writing gift was passed down from you (with the other half from Mummy because we know she can talk!). My fondest memories are of you taking me to secondary school at the start of each school term, mummy and I laughing at you and your love of food. I am ever so grateful to God for you. You are a constant reminder of the compassion and mercies of God. We celebrate your recovery, we rejoice in your healing and thank God for His hand that is firmly upon your life.

Finally, to my mother, my sweet, strong mother, Felicia Amaefuna. What can I say? You are an inspiration! Your strength and determination is extraordinary and exemplary. I have seen you defeat (twice!) a life-threatening illness that kills women half your age to the surprise and amazement of doctors. I have watched you care for your husband when illness struck despite undergoing treatment yourself. I have seen you press on in the face of obstacle after obstacle, refusing to give up or quit! Your love for your children and your husband is second to none! When I look at my life and how far I come, I know that some of those qualities I see and admire in you are the same ones that have brought me thus far. You always used to call me 'Daddy's Girl' but I am also very much my 'Mother's Daughter'. Your time of rest is now! The Lord has seen your tears and all that you have lost, and He will surely reward your labour of love.

I love you all!

Acknowledgements

My journey to this point has been interesting and well, nothing short of amazing, but I wouldn't have been able to get here without the love and support of those around me. I need to say thank you to my friend, partner, and darling husband, Gbadero, a man of such faith, who has shown me what it truly means to dare to live your dreams and love God passionately. Gbadero, thank you for leading by example and challenging me to be the best me that I can be. I didn't always appreciate your persistence, but I am most grateful for it.

I also want to thank my best friend, my confidante and my sister in every sense of the word, a friend who has supported me tirelessly and faithfully on this journey, through her words and in her actions. Ndidi: thank you for refusing to allow me to give up, for spurring me on and for believing in me relentlessly, every step of the way.

The acknowledgements would not be complete if I did not extend my appreciation and gratitude to my pastors from House on the Rock, The London Lighthouse—Pastors Michael and Carol Efueye. You both are a true reflection of what it means to imitate Christ. Your down-to-earth leadership, wisdom, and integrity have been pivotal in my spiritual growth and contributed to the woman that I am today.

A sincere thanks, to all who have been on this journey with me in some form or the other, through your words of support and encouragement.

Last and by no means the least, I am grateful to God, the Giver of the gift, the One who makes a way when there seems to be no way and without whom this book would not have been possible. You see the best in me when I cannot see it in myself. You remain faithful even when I am not and for that, I am eternally grateful.

Foreword

In these difficult and perilous times facing the world, where there is so much pain, disappointment and disillusionment, there is nothing more valuable for Christians than a book full of reassuring words of faith, hope and encouragement.

This book comes highly recommended as an excellent constant companion for Christians and non-believers alike, as we face the daily battles and onslaught of the devil's attack on our minds, spirits, bodies and souls.

Whether you are on a train, a bus, a plane, on your lunch break, or even during your quiet time, it is a reservoir of scriptures and words that can immediately cause your spirit to soar, bringing to your remembrance the promises of God, His omnipotence and beneficence and setting you back on the right path for victorious living.

Be blessed as you read.

Carol Efueye.

Introduction

The biggest mistake we make as Christians is to believe (knowingly or unknowingly) that we will not go through difficult times. Giving control of your life over to Christ does not exempt you from life's challenges; it simply guarantees you help in times of distress. Shortly, before His death, Jesus warned His disciples that they would face tests and troubles but they should not be discouraged or filled with fear because He had overcome the world (John 16:33).

Your faith in Jesus Christ and His death on the cross is your guarantee that whatever you are going through will pass. The Bible says in 1 John 5:4-5, 'For every child of God defeats this evil world and we achieve this victory through our faith. And who can win this battle against the world? Only those who believe that Jesus is the Son of God.'

In my relationship with God, I have encountered some difficult periods and there were times when I would cry out to God in bewilderment and anger, wondering what was happening and why. At other times, feelings of discouragement and apathy would assail me; however, I have come to learn and understand that God loves me, and He is Sovereign! This means that He has a purpose and plan of which I am a part, and His methods for achieving His plans are not always comfortable or understood.

You may be going through challenges now and have given up hope that your circumstances will change. This might be because the issue has persisted for so long. For some of you it might be as a result of a wrong decision and for others, maybe there is no battle being fought; you are at a crossroads in your life and simply dissatisfied with where you are. You are stuck in a rut or the proverbial 'rat race', but want more out of life. Whatever your particular situation, this book is intended to show God's heart towards you. For every problem or predicament He already gave you a Word so that you would enjoy life to the full. Christ died to give you an abundant life here on earth and not when you get to heaven!

If you are feeling a sense of hopelessness, there are messages of faith to give you hope; if you are struggling with low self-esteem, God wants you to know that you are precious and valuable in His sight. If you are feeling unfulfilled and disenchanted with life, you were created for a purpose and endowed with gifts and talents to fulfil that purpose. Wherever you are, whatever your need, there is a message from the throne room just for you!

Read and be empowered!

This Thing Called Faith . . .

'. . . For assuredly, I say to you, if you have faith as a mustard
seed, you will say to this mountain, 'Move from here to there,'
and it will move; and nothing will be impossible for you.'
(Matt. 17:20)

Against All Odds!

Romans 4:17-21, The Message

We call Abraham 'father' not because he got God's attention by living like a saint, but because God made something out of Abraham when he was a nobody ... When everything was hopeless, Abraham believed anyway, deciding to live not on the basis of what he saw he couldn't do but on what God said he would do. And so he was made father of a multitude of peoples. God himself said to him, 'You're going to have a big family, Abraham!' Abraham didn't focus on his own impotence and say, 'It's hopeless. This hundred-year-old body could never father a child.' Nor did he survey Sarah's decades of infertility and give up. He didn't tiptoe around God's promise asking cautiously sceptical questions. He plunged into the promise and came up strong, ready for God, sure that God would make good on what he had said.

I love this scripture because as clichéd as it sounds, it gives me hope and reminds me that with God all things are possible, if you believe (Mark 9:23, paraphrased).

God gave Abraham the promise of a son from his seed and via Sarah's womb at the age of seventy-five. Given that they had been childless for seventy-five years, you'd think that the moment the promise was given, Sarah would have conceived immediately and a bouncing baby boy would bounce right into their lives, but no such luck. It was to be another twenty-five years before Abraham saw the fulfilment of that promise.

The thing that humbles me about this story is that a childless Abraham followed God wholeheartedly at seventy-five years old before the promise was given, and still continued to serve and believe God for many years before the promise was fulfilled. In all that time Abraham didn't sit around and lament at the hopelessness of his situation. He didn't question God's ability to deliver on His promise by entertaining doubts; he just believed and continued to believe. Faith is active and constant. It doesn't stop when the promise is given; it continues until the manifestation.

Another translation (NKJV) says, 'He did not consider his own body, already dead (since he was about a hundred years old), and the deadness of Sarah's womb'. The dictionary definition of 'consider' is' to fix the mind on, with a view to a careful examination; to think on with care; to ponder; to study; to meditate on'. Abraham gave no thought to his physical body but chose to focus on the Words of the One whose Word is forever settled, the One who created the universe with His Words and upholds the universe with the power of those same words.

Jesus in talking to His disciples said, 'There are some things that people cannot do, but God can do anything' (Matt. 19:26, CEV). The story of Abraham was written for our admonition and encouragement. God is limitless, but we limit our blessings by placing boundaries on what God can and cannot do. Abraham didn't allow any room for doubt but was fully convinced that what God had promised, He was able to perform! How convinced are you that what God has vowed to give you He is more than able to bring it to pass?

God's Word—The Final Say

James 1:6-8, Contemporary English Version

But when you ask for something, you must have faith and not doubt. Anyone who doubts is like an ocean wave tossed around in a storm. If you are that kind of person, you can't make up your mind, and you surely can't be trusted. So don't expect the Lord to give you anything at all.

I was talking to God one morning—or to be more accurate—interrogating Him and His reasons for why certain things were the way they were. That morning, the Holy Spirit revealed to me with such clarity accustomed to the third person of the Trinity that I do not trust God as much as I think or proclaim to. This is a feeling I am sure many people can identify with. You cry out to God in times of trouble and reach the skewed conclusion that maybe God doesn't speak, or if He does, He doesn't speak to you. Well, let me correct that misguided theology—God does speak, but He responds to words of faith not fear!

The reason for your unrest and uncertainty where some decisions are concerned is that you don't trust God as much as you ought or profess to. So much so, that when troubles assail you, you are easily moved. The true test of what you believe is how you respond when things happen that are contrary to what God has spoken. The substance of your belief is tested when troubles come—how do you react? Do you stand on God's Word and declare you will not be moved by what your eyes can see, or do you panic and start to consider your options? Jerry Savelle gave a beautiful description of faithfulness (from which the root word 'faith' is derived)—'Faithfulness is sticking with God and His Word no matter what happens in life'. How faithful are you to the things God has told you? If He told you that you would buy a house this year, have you started looking at properties in areas you like? Have you investigated the different types of home loans? Have you seen a financial advisor to find out how much you can borrow? They may tell you, you don't have enough: well that's fine because your Father is Jehovah El-Shaddai, the all-sufficient God!

Your ability to remain faithful in the face of setbacks is the true mark of faith. Stop questioning why things are the way they are and thank God because He is working everything (even the unpleasant things) out for your good. Faith is a conscious decision to ignore everything that does not line up with the Word of God and make His Word the final say in every matter. Your response to every contrary situation in life must be God said it, and I believe it irrespective of how things appear. There is always darkness before light; sickness before healing; lack before abundance; but faith in God is where it all begins and ends!

Faith Is . . .

Hebrews 11:1, New Living Translation

Faith is the confidence that what we hope for will actually happen; it gives us assurance about things we cannot see.

The Amplified Version of the Bible says, 'NOW FAITH is the assurance (the confirmation, the title deed) of the things [we] hope for, being the proof of things [we] do not see and the conviction of their reality [faith perceiving as real fact what is not revealed to the senses]'.

This is a difficult concept to grasp. I mean, how can faith be evidence or the proof of that which we cannot see? That is the first mistake we make as human beings when trying to understand the ways of God. We try to attach human understanding and reasoning to the things of the spirit, but the things of the spirit cannot be explained with human logic and reasoning. I mean what would make a man build an ark when he had never seen rain nor know what rain was? What would make a little shepherd boy believe he could kill a giant with a mere stone, or a man to take his family, leave his home, and go to a land he didn't know? All these men had one thing in common—they had faith, but not just any kind of faith; they had faith in God!

Many of you have big dreams that just don't seem possible in your strength with your current qualifications, abilities and status. God has given you certain instructions, but they just don't make sense, so instead of moving you are trying to work it out. For some of us, we are waiting for God to confirm what He has already told us and in some cases we are waiting for the next instruction, wondering why God hasn't spoken. He won't speak until you act on the last instruction He gave you. What was the last thing He told you? Have you obeyed it?

Faith is stepping out in the confident knowledge that God has a good plan for your life and He will make provision for your every need, every step of the way. As you take that first step, you train yourself in trust and God will give you the next instruction, making the path clearer.

'Your faith will always meet a mountain of evidence that seems to contradict God's Word', but you must believe God no matter how real your situation appears to be. His Word is the yardstick. Real faith is accepting it without seeing the evidence of it.

Have Faith in God

Mark 11:22, New Living Translation

Then Jesus said to the disciples, 'Have faith in God'.

The Amplified Version of the Bible says, 'And Jesus, replying, said to them, Have faith in God [constantly]', meaning we need faith for every moment, every day. Faith is not something you have today but don't have tomorrow. It doesn't have an *on-off* switch.

Kenneth E. Hagin once said, 'Faith begins where the will of God is known!'[1] You might be thinking, well obviously, so what's the great revelation? Well, for me this was a fresh look at faith. Oftentimes, when we are trusting God for something, we say we have faith, but really what we have is hope. Consequently, when the thing we are praying about doesn't materialise, we begin to doubt and get discouraged. In some cases, despair and desperation set in and we begin to question God's love for us. We resort to feeling sorry for ourselves and then begin to resent God and others who have what we want, but this stems from a lack of knowledge and understanding.

Let me explain. You need £500 and you believe that your father will give it to you even though you haven't asked him for it, and he hasn't made any commitment to give it to you. That is hope. Now if your father specifically tells you that he will give you the money either verbally or in writing (in the case of a will), then you can exercise faith because there is an agreement in place, which lets you know that the money is yours. Likewise, oftentimes, we hold on to scriptures and profess to have faith concerning a matter without knowing what God's will is concerning that thing. We declare, confess, receive, apprehend, bind and lose all in an attempt to exercise our faith and somehow, call forth the things we want. We are all on different journeys, so just because it worked for James does not mean it will work for Samantha.

Before you can have faith, you must know the will of God in that situation. Some things are 'easier' to have faith for because God's will is quite clear. For example, God's will with respect to sickness is healing, full stop! There is no debate or uncertainty here; the Bible categorically states in Isaiah 53:5 that, 'By His stripes you are healed!' Other things are not as clear-cut and therefore you have to spend time seeking it out by studying His Word and spending time in prayer.

When the will of God is known, then you can boldly declare you have faith and stand confidently in that faith, even when everything around you is contrary. You will be able to remain steadfast in the face of ridicule and disbelief from others because you are operating from a place of revelation. It is then that your faith has the substance described in Hebrews 11:1 because there is a confidence you have which arises from the knowledge that this is God's will.

Seeing Isn't Believing

2 Corinthians 5:7, New Living Translation

For we live by believing and not by seeing.

As human beings, we are governed by our five senses—touch, sight, smell, hearing and taste, and these senses dictate how we respond to certain situations. You would have heard of the popular saying 'Seeing is believing'. In other words, when you see, then you believe. That is how the world operates; however, as spiritual beings, we are governed by faith, which means that we are not led by our physical senses. We approach each situation with the eyes of faith (spiritual insight).

When faced with trouble, we adopt God's perspective—what does God's Word say about the situation? For example, when faced with sickness, our response is not acceptance but confession of healing—'The Lord forgives our sins, heals us when we are sick . . .' (Ps. 103:3, CEV). When faced with lack, the truth is you shall not want for anything because 'the Lord is your Shepherd, you will never be in need' (Ps. 23:1, CEV). When troubles afflict you, the Bible says, 'Many are the afflictions of the righteous, but the Lord delivers him out of them all' (Ps. 34:19).

Walking by faith is not easy, but it is necessary. The more we work our faith, the stronger our faith becomes. What you see becomes your reality. If all you see is the hopelessness of your situation, that's all it will ever be. God instructs us to walk by faith because in so doing we change our circumstances. In other words, God is saying, don't worry about what the situation looks like in the natural, I have the power to change the situation and I will; all you have to do is believe that I can and confess with your mouth what you believe! It's not enough to believe it in your heart; you have to speak it with your mouth.

Faith is the leaning of your entire being on God in total confidence in His power and love for you, knowing that God is with you and He will never leave you no matter how bad things get. He is the friend who sticks with you when the going is good and sticks even closer when the going gets rough. He doesn't abandon you when things are bad; He carries you! Trust God; not what your eyes can see or what you feel—'So we don't look at the troubles we can see now; rather, we fix our gaze on things that cannot be seen. For the things we see now will soon be gone, but the things we cannot see will last forever' (2 Cor. 4:18). So, walk by faith and not by what you can see!

seek Him'. This woman approached Jesus, believing that He was the Son of God and that He was able to heal her. Her faith was rewarded with healing and complete restoration.

Contrary to what some people say and believe, sickness is not God's will. His desire is that you live an abundant (fruitful and joyful) life—'The thief does not come except to steal, and to kill, and to destroy. I have come that they may have life, and that they may have it more abundantly' (John 10:10, NKJV). Anything that does not represent 'life' is not of God. Sickness is not from God. He doesn't put sickness upon you to teach you something, and He does not get glory from sickness. You need to renew your mind with the truth of God's Word, which says you are healed and then access the healing that is rightfully yours. You are healed!

A Touch Is All You Need

Mark 5:28-29, New Living Translation

For she thought to herself, 'If I can just touch his robe, I will be healed.' Immediately the bleeding stopped, and she could feel in her body that she had been healed of her terrible condition.

Most people have heard of the story of the woman with the issue of blood and interestingly, we are not told her name. Why? Because it doesn't matter. What's important is that she had an issue, which had been going on for several years. This woman could be anyone who has been in a situation or condition that has persisted for far too long.

This woman had seen many physicians, but none of them were able to help her. I imagine she must have reached the point of desperation and decided that her situation had to change. She had probably heard about the many miracles Jesus had performed and decided that if she could just touch Him, it would be enough to rid her of the ailment, which had ravaged her body for twelve years and restore her to health. The moment she touched His garment, she was healed instantly. There was something different about her touch that made her stand out from the touch of the crowd pressing against Jesus. She touched Him with determination, intent on receiving her healing. How do I know she was determined? She had suffered from this condition for so long that most people in her shoes would have given up and accepted that there was no cure. But not her! She refused to quit and made her way to Jesus despite the throbbing crowd.

Jesus was on His way to heal the daughter of Jairus, the leader of the synagogue, when this woman put her faith into action. Her faith pleased God. It is not enough to call on God, but you must also believe He is able to do that which you are seeking of Him. The Bible says in Hebrews 11:6, NLT, 'And it is impossible to please God without faith. Anyone who wants to come to Him must believe that God exists and that He rewards those who sincerely seek Him'. This woman approached Jesus, believing that He was the Son of God and that He was able to heal her. Her faith was rewarded with healing and complete restoration.

Contrary to what some people say and believe, sickness is not God's will. His desire is that you live an abundant (fruitful and joyful) life—'The thief does not come except to steal, and to kill, and to destroy. I have come that they may have life, and that they may have it more abundantly' (John 10:10, NKJV). Anything that does not represent 'life' is not of God. Sickness is not from God. He doesn't put sickness upon you to teach you something, and He does not get glory from sickness. You need to renew your mind with the truth of God's Word, which says you are healed and then access the healing that is rightfully yours. You are healed!

What Do You Want from Him?

Matthew 20:30-34, New International Version

Two blind men were sitting by the roadside, and when they heard that Jesus was going by, they shouted, 'Lord, Son of David, have mercy on us!' The crowd rebuked them and told them to be quiet, but they shouted all the louder, 'Lord, Son of David, have mercy on us!' Jesus stopped and called them. 'What do you want me to do for you?' he asked. 'Lord,' they answered, 'we want our sight.' Jesus had compassion on them and touched their eyes. Immediately they received their sight and followed him.

There is the misconception even amongst some Christians that healing isn't for everybody, that it is God's will for some to be healed and others not to be. This is a controversial topic, and I am not going to pretend to have all the answers. However, my own conviction regarding the topic of healing stems from my personal understanding of what is written in the Bible.

1 Peter 2:24, NKJV, says, 'who Himself bore our sins in His own body on the tree, that we, having died to sins, might live for righteousness—by whose stripes you were healed.' Notice the words 'were healed'. Healing is not something that is going to happen some time in the future. We are healed because Jesus paid the price on the cross by virtue of the whipping He endured at the hands of the Roman soldiers.

For a lot of people, this is a hard concept to get their head around. Even as I write, there are some diseases that come to mind and I am like, really? A person can be healed from that? Where are the children of faith who truly believe that all things are possible with God? The three blind men didn't care what the people thought. They needed help and recognised that Jesus was the only one who could help them. When they saw Jesus passing by, they cried out to Him for help. Interestingly, Jesus responds by asking them, 'What do you want from Me?' Hmmm . . . surely it's obvious. Hang on! Aren't you meant to be Omniscient? They are blind. They want to see.

On reading the Bible, I noticed from other instances of Jesus's interaction with people is that He asks questions when He wants to expose what is in their heart, what they really think and believe. Do you really want to be healed? Do you believe that Jesus has healed you? People will tell you to be quiet, that healing isn't for everyone or that perhaps it's not God's will in that particular situation. Well, I disagree. I can't explain why some people don't get better, but if you are reading this now, God's will is that you are healed. James 5:15, CEV, says, 'If you have faith when you pray for sick people, they will get well. The Lord will heal them . . .' Psalm 41:3, NLT, says, 'The Lord nurses them when they are sick and restores them to health'.

Jesus is the same yesterday, today and forever (Heb. 13:8). His Word concerning healing has not changed and will never change. Healing is a part of the finished work as is salvation. Jesus didn't die so that you could have one and not the other. When you make Him Lord of your life, you receive everything that pertains to life and godliness, which includes healing and wholeness.

He Is Your Healer!

Psalm 103:2-3, New King James Version

Let all that I am praise the Lord; may I never forget the good things He does for me. He forgives all my sins and heals all my diseases.

There are so many scriptures on healing that it's hard to believe that people are still unsure as to whether it is their entitlement or not. How is it that we can believe God forgives our sins, but in the very same breath question whether He heals all diseases? God is not the author of confusion (1 Cor. 14:33, NKJV), so we need to go back to the drawing board.

You may be thinking it's easy for me to say; after all, I've never been in a situation that was so hopeless . . . Well, that's where you're wrong. I watched God bring my father from the jaws of death because a group of people joined faith and believed God when He said we are healed. The doctors said he would not make it and asked us to prepare for the worst. That night, as he lay dying in the hospital, a priest was called to perform last rites over him in readiness for his death, but thank God for faithful friends who believed in the promises of God. In that same hospital, my friends and I gathered round my father's bed, and holding hands we prayed. As we prayed, we laid hands on him for the Bible says, 'And these signs will follow those who believe . . . they will lay hands on the sick and they will recover' (Mark 16:17-18, NKJV). Jesus wasn't just talking to the disciples; He was referring to anyone that would believe in Him. You don't have to wait for a pastor, bishop or priest to lay hands on you or a loved one. The spirit of God in them is the same spirit in you. Lay hands on yourself and speak the Word of God over your life and health. God's Word cannot return to Him void (Isa. 55:11). Four years later, my father is still with us against all medical odds.

I have seen a friend survive a brain aneurysm and the subsequent operation when specialists in the medical field said she wouldn't make it. When the news came, we prayed constantly, and without ceasing, thanking God for her healing by virtue of the shed blood of Jesus Christ. The Bible tells us that '... The earnest prayer of a righteous person has great power and produces wonderful results' (James 5:16, NLT). We saw those results—my friend walked away from the jaws of death, which the doctors had described as imminent. The doctors' report was that she would die, but she lived! The doctors said she would be in intensive care for one week; she was out in twenty-four hours. They said she wouldn't be able to function as she used to and that she would need months and months of rehabilitation, but within two months of being discharged from the hospital she was doing all the things she used to do. The promises of God (including healing) are 'Yes' and 'Amen' (2 Cor. 1:20) and are available to whosoever believes.

The doctors may say there is no hope, but God says, '... I am the Lord who heals you' (Exod. 15:26, NLT). Whose report will you believe?

Courage in the Face of Fear . . .

'Fear not, for I am with you; be not dismayed, for I am
your God. I will strengthen you, Yes, I will help you, I
will uphold you with My righteous right hand.'
(Isa. 41:10)

Do It Afraid

2 Kings 7:3-8, The Message

Now there were four men with leprosy sitting at the entrance of the city gates. 'Why should we sit here waiting to die?' they asked each other. 'We will starve if we stay here, but with the famine in the city, we will starve if we go back there. So we might as well go out and surrender to the Syrian army. If they let us live, so much the better. But if they kill us, we would have died anyway.' So at twilight they set out for the camp of the Syrians. But when they came to the edge of the camp, no one was there! For the Lord had caused the Syrian army to hear the clatter of speeding chariots and the galloping of horses and the sounds of a great army approaching . . . So they panicked and ran into the night, abandoning their tents, horses, donkeys, and everything else, as they fled for their lives. When the lepers arrived at the edge of the camp, they went into one tent after another, eating and drinking wine; and they carried off silver and gold and clothing and hid it.

We live in a world where change is the order of the day; where quick solutions and quick wins are required instantly. If a problem exists, a solution is not far behind in the form of science or technology. People (including Christians) rely on the created rather than the Creator; some go through life believing that there is no solution to their particular problem and that the best thing to do is give up and accept whatever circumstances they find themselves in. Many of us have more faith in our bank managers and doctors, who are here today and gone tomorrow, than the God, who is the same yesterday, today and forever!

Stories such as that of the four lepers are written not to entertain, but rather to challenge us. The lepers were faced with a difficult decision; if they remained where they were, they would starve to death and if they went back to the city, there was a very good chance that they would die from the famine. The only other option was to surrender themselves to the enemy and again they faced the possibility of death. In spite of their obvious limitations, the

Courage in the Face of Fear . . .

'Fear not, for I am with you; be not dismayed, for I am
your God. I will strengthen you, Yes, I will help you, I
will uphold you with My righteous right hand.'
(Isa. 41:10)

Be Bold and Courageous

Joshua 1:9, New King James Version

'Have I not commanded you? Be strong and of good courage; do not be afraid, nor be dismayed, for the LORD your God is with you wherever you go.'

Following the death of Moses, God appointed Joshua as the new leader of the Israelites and instructed him to lead the people into the Promised Land. When faced with this task, Joshua felt inadequate in light of his predecessor, Moses. He didn't feel qualified to do what the Lord was asking him to do. Three times in the first book of Joshua, God instructs Joshua to be strong and courageous. Why? Because following God does not exempt you from troubles or situations that require you to step out of your comfort zone. In instructing Joshua, God was telling him not to give into the fear or discouragement that would surely come because God is with him.

Each of us has been endowed with certain talents and abilities for a specific purpose. Many of us have ideas we desire to make tangible, but for some reason, we are either too scared or too comfortable where we are to take the first step. To accomplish great things, requires boldness and courage even in the face of your fear. God wants to demonstrate His enabling power (grace) in your life, but the degree to which He can operate is dependent on you taking that first step.

Stepping out in boldness does not mean that you will be exempt from challenges. Obstacles will still present themselves, but the rewards are much greater than if you just remained where you were. When you step out, you will face doubt and thoughts will arise, making you question whether you heard God in the first place. You will encounter moments of uncertainty, fear and discouragement, but God will never leave you without help, for God said, 'I will never fail you. I will never abandon you' (Heb. 13:5, NLT). He has already gone ahead of you and made provision for that which He is asking you to do. He left you with His Word and the Holy Spirit to guide and direct you.

He also left you with examples in the Bible of everyday people like you who faced similar challenges and came through them. Courage is not the absence of fear—it is doing what you know you must do in spite of the fear!

Be bold and courageous; step out this year, knowing that God is with you wherever you go!

Do It Afraid

2 Kings 7:3-8, The Message

Now there were four men with leprosy sitting at the entrance of the city gates. 'Why should we sit here waiting to die?' they asked each other. 'We will starve if we stay here, but with the famine in the city, we will starve if we go back there. So we might as well go out and surrender to the Syrian army. If they let us live, so much the better. But if they kill us, we would have died anyway.' So at twilight they set out for the camp of the Syrians. But when they came to the edge of the camp, no one was there! For the Lord had caused the Syrian army to hear the clatter of speeding chariots and the galloping of horses and the sounds of a great army approaching ... So they panicked and ran into the night, abandoning their tents, horses, donkeys, and everything else, as they fled for their lives. When the lepers arrived at the edge of the camp, they went into one tent after another, eating and drinking wine; and they carried off silver and gold and clothing and hid it.

We live in a world where change is the order of the day; where quick solutions and quick wins are required instantly. If a problem exists, a solution is not far behind in the form of science or technology. People (including Christians) rely on the created rather than the Creator; some go through life believing that there is no solution to their particular problem and that the best thing to do is give up and accept whatever circumstances they find themselves in. Many of us have more faith in our bank managers and doctors, who are here today and gone tomorrow, than the God, who is the same yesterday, today and forever!

Stories such as that of the four lepers are written not to entertain, but rather to challenge us. The lepers were faced with a difficult decision; if they remained where they were, they would starve to death and if they went back to the city, there was a very good chance that they would die from the famine. The only other option was to surrender themselves to the enemy and again they faced the possibility of death. In spite of their obvious limitations, the lepers wisely came to the understanding that either way they could die, but there was a possibility that they might live if they stepped out, whereas they had more to lose if they remained where they were.

Life is all about choices. Sometimes the safest thing to do is to stay where you are, but the safest thing to do is not always the wisest or right thing to do! Each of us was created with specific talents and abilities for a specific purpose. Don't let fear or comfort prevent you from taking that step. You will never know what could have been until you make that move.

In life, we take risks in the hope that the outcome will be favourable, but inevitably, we win some and we lose some. However, with God, there is no such thing as a miscalculated risk; you win every time. View challenges as channels for God's glory and your limitations as ladders to unbelievable heights of blessing! The amazing thing about the leper's situation is that they were literally at the entrance to the gate of the city. The distance between you and your breakthrough is a single act of courage.

Ding-Dong, Goliath Is Dead!

1 Samuel 17:37, 45, New Living Translation

The Lord who rescued me from the claws of the lion and the bear will rescue me from this Philistine!' . . . David replied to the Philistine, 'You come to me with sword, spear, and javelin, but I come to you in the name of the Lord of Heaven's Armies—the God of the armies of Israel, whom you have defied.

There are times in life when we find ourselves in unpleasant situations or come up against obstacles to our progress, and the fear of failure or defeat causes us to run away. In this story, the obstacle in the way of the Israelites victory was a giant named Goliath. After reading the description of Goliath, quite frankly, I could sympathise with the Israelites retreating in fear. If I had been in their shoes, honestly, I think I might have approached Goliath with a white flag and said 'just kill me now!' Everything about Goliath from the crown of his head to the soles of his feet was a hazard warning, which screamed giant on the prowl, approach at your own peril!

Now there was a shepherd boy called David who was small in comparison to all the other men of Israel, and yet he was the only one brave enough to take on Goliath. In fact, when you read the story, David was incensed that a Philistine would dare to come against the children of the Most High God. This level of confidence could only come from someone who knew who he was, but more importantly, knew who his God was! It was this confidence in God that enabled David to boldly go up against Goliath with simply a sling and five stones. When you look at it, it doesn't make sense. It is sheer madness and inconceivable that David could kill Goliath, given his stature and weapons of choice. The odds were so clearly stacked against David, but God loves it when the odds are against you because then there can be no doubt in anybody's mind that the victory belongs to God.

David called to remembrance all the times God had delivered him from other treacherous situations. To him, if God could deliver him from the jaws of a lion and the claws of a bear, then killing Goliath was a walk in the park! David showed no fear; he was confident that he would kill Goliath because he rightly understood that God and him were the majority.

This story illustrates that no situation, no matter how big is insurmountable because 'if God be for us, who can be against us?' (Rom. 8:31, NKJV) Saul gave David his armour to wear, but David chose not to wear it because it was uncomfortable, and as a shepherd boy, he was not used to wearing such attire. David was comfortable with his simple slingshot, a weapon he was skilled at using. God will use the unique gifts and talents He has placed on the inside of you. So what is that thing or those things you have in your hand that you have taken for granted? You will never know what you are capable of achieving until you give God what is in your hand. You are just one slingshot from experiencing the fullness of what God has prepared for you!

Walking on Water

Matthew 14:27-31, New Living Translation

But Jesus spoke to them at once. 'Don't be afraid,' he said. 'Take courage. I am here!' Then Peter called to him, 'Lord, if it's really you, tell me to come to you, walking on the water.' 'Yes come', Jesus said. So Peter went over the side of the boat and walked on the water towards Jesus. But when he saw the strong wind and the waves, he was terrified and began to sink. 'Save me, Lord!' he shouted. Jesus immediately reached out and grabbed him. 'You have so little faith,' Jesus said. 'Why did you doubt me?'

Peter gets bad press for walking on water and then suddenly sinking, but he deserves a lot of credit because at least he stepped out. The other disciples watched from the safety of the boat while Peter dared to do what no one else had the courage to do. While the other disciples remained as spectators of the incredible, Peter was doing the unthinkable. Such people are governed by fear, but fear is not of God. This is no different from present day. You have those who do and those who watch those who do. You can't afford to be a mere bystander while life passes you by; too afraid to leave the comfort of that job, too afraid to venture into the unknown, and too afraid to try and fail. You are not a failure if you fail; you are a failure when you stop trying! We are imperfect people, and there will be times when we fail, but those times are an opportunity for growth and a healthy reminder that we must depend on God, not ourselves.

The fact that Peter even dared to walk on the water is truly amazing, and he was doing so well until he took his eyes of Jesus and began to focus on what was going on around him. The moment he did that, fear took over, and he began to sink. This is the situation a lot of us find ourselves in today. We step out in faith based on an instruction from God, and then we encounter an obstacle, become flustered, and begin to 'sink'. You can guarantee that when God gives you a Word, that Word will be tried and tested to see if you truly believe what you have heard. When trouble comes on account of the Word we receive, we take our eyes off God and start to focus on the situation at hand. Panic and fear set in, and we begin to doubt that we even heard God in the first place. Fear is contrary to faith and opens the door to doubt, discouragement, and defeat. Don't give any room to fear. The moment you feel fear, *speak* the Word of God, for the Bible says, 'For God has not given us a spirit of fear and timidity, but of power, love, and self-discipline' (2 Tim. 1:7, NLT). The Message translation says, 'God doesn't want us to be shy with his gifts, but bold and loving and sensible.'

The beauty of this story is that even though Peter wavered and slipped, Jesus caught him. If you step out and fall, God will catch you! Despite this incident and many others subsequently where Peter retreated in fear, God still used him to build the church. Fear often makes us seek further confirmation from God when we should be taking action. 'Walking on Water' or doing the impossible requires you to face your fear and keep your focus fixed on God as you navigate the storms of life.

Where Do You Stand?

Daniel 3:17-18, New Living Translation

'If we are thrown into the blazing furnace, the God whom we serve is able to save us. He will rescue us from your power, Your Majesty. But even if he doesn't, we want to make it clear to you, Your Majesty, that we will never serve your gods or worship the gold statue you have set up.'

Many of us are familiar with the story of Shadrach, Meshach, and Abed-Nego, who were thrown into a burning furnace of fire because they refused to denounce God and bow down to worship an idol. These men were faced with a choice—give into fear or take a stand for God. They took a stand for God and were thrown 'alive' into a furnace of fire (the dictionary definition of furnace is 'a place characterised by intense heat') and walked out unscathed! I think we underestimate the enormity and sheer power of the miracle. Such was the intensity of the heat from the fire that it killed the soldiers who threw the three men in; however, the three Hebrews boys in the midst of the fire remained untouched.

Some of the challenges you are facing have nothing to do with the devil and everything to do with God. From this story we see that Shadrach, Meshach and Abed-Nego didn't just profess to know God; they knew God! When faced with the very real threat of death for refusing to worship the idol erected by Nebuchadnezzar, they stood their ground. They were confident that God would rescue them, and if for some reason, He didn't, He is Sovereign and knows best.

We would have expected God to intercede before the men were thrown into the fire. Perhaps a flash of lightening that would incinerate Nebuchadnezzar and his entire army, but not so. Their deliverance came in the midst of the test. In times of hardship, there are really only two options—'fight the good fight of faith' (1 Tim. 6:12, NKJV) or surrender to your fear. Notice that the first option involves you taking action while the latter requires no effort but simply to give in.

There comes a time when we must say, 'If I perish, I perish', and if I perish, I know that God is with me. Too many of us still have options—we run to doctors, bank managers, mortgage brokers, pastors, and even friends. When none of them can help, then, as a last resort, we 'try' God. God is not a Plan B, C, or D! Perhaps God has not shown up in your situation yet because you still have a back-up plan. How confident are you in God's ability to come through for you? Can you trust God even when you can't see Him? When your faith is put to the test, do you boldly declare God's promises or do you cower in fear and give into the pressure? If you want to see a miraculous move of God in your furnace of affliction, let your report be like that of the three Hebrew boys: 'our God whom we serve is able to deliver us!'

Searching for Purpose . . .

'For we are God's [own] handiwork (His workmanship), recreated in
Christ Jesus, [born anew] that we may do those good works which
God predestined (planned beforehand) for us [taking paths which
He prepared ahead of time], that we should walk in them [living the
good life which He prearranged and made ready for us to live].'
(Eph. 2:10)

Do You Have a Dream?

Isaiah 43:18-19, New King James Version

Do not [earnestly] remember the former things; neither consider the things of old. Behold, I am doing a new thing! Now it springs forth; do you not perceive and know it and will you not give heed to it? I will even make a way in the wilderness and rivers in the desert.

We all have a duty to pursue the dreams God has placed on the inside of us. Many of us get discouraged and give up because we can't see how it's going to work. The 'how' is not for you to worry about. Yours is not to work out how it will happen, your responsibility is to pursue the dream or vision with faith, trusting that God will make a way.

Sometimes, you are not meant to finish the vision but initiate it and pass the baton on to the next generation to continue. This is what the likes of Rosa Parks, Martin Luther King, and President Barack Obama have done or are doing. Martin Luther King did not see his dream come to pass before his death, but he was assured by his faith in God to do the impossible, that it would be fulfilled. He kick-started the process, which is what a leader does—he stands in the gap for others. The injustices suffered by so many generations before us no longer seem in vain. Obama has achieved what no one in his generation, the generation before or even our generation ever thought possible! For many, he has given hope; for some, he has restored their faith in humanity; and for others, he has shown that change truly is possible if one believes and is passionate enough.

What are those dreams that are burning on the inside of you or ideas that seem crazy? Look around you—people are making an impact and leaving a mark on this generation and the generations to come. Don't get so consumed with wealth and material things that you leave this earth without leaving an impact. When you get to heaven, God will not ask how many cars you bought or how much profit your business made. He is not interested in how many houses you built or owned, or how many qualifications you amassed. He will ask you what you did with the precious gifts and ideas He put on the inside of you. He will ask you how many lives were made better because of you. Most precious of all gifts is the gift of time. It is given to everyone in the same quantity. What are you doing with your time? Time is a non-renewable resource—once it is gone, you can't get it back.

God is doing a new thing—will you be a participator or a spectator?

Created to Succeed

Jeremiah 1:5, New Living Translation

'I knew you before I formed you in your mother's womb. Before you were born I set you apart . . .'

Before a manufacturer creates a product, they have a picture in mind of what the product should look like and what purpose it has been designed to fill. So it is with man. God had a vision that led Him to create you. You have heard it so many times; you are not here by accident or by chance! You are not here to just exist or occupy space. God has a purpose for you and until you discover what that is and start walking in it you will not find true fulfilment. Until we become the reason why we were created, the vision God has for us cannot be fulfilled.

God created us in His very own image, which means that we have what it takes to succeed. We have authority and dominion in any land we place our feet whether it is the UK, Africa, the United States, or anywhere else. When God created man, He called us blessed, which means you are 'empowered to prosper'. Your prosperity is not tied to anyone or any place; your prosperity is tied to you so why are you chasing prosperity? Why are you looking for what you already have? Rather seek His will, seek His very reason for creating you. Those gifts and talents are for use in the Kingdom. Matthew 6:33, CEV, states, 'But more than anything else, put God's work first and do what He wants then the other things will be yours as well.' You are a solution to a problem. Find the problem and be the solution! Your question to God should be, 'What did You have in mind for me at creation?'

God does not start something He hasn't already finished. In other words, at the time of creation, all that you would ever need to succeed was put on the inside of you, and our daily walk with Christ is a revealing of what has already been done. Picture a wedding album. You start at the beginning with the bride getting ready, then you progress to the pictures of her arriving at the church, but it doesn't end there. During the course of the day, pictures will be added to the album—pictures of the ceremony, the reception, the honeymoon, children, and so on and so forth. So it is with our lives. This is not your end; this is merely one shot of many slides!

We need to lay down our lives to Him, not in our words but in our actions. We have to trust God because His ways are perfect. Don't let money or fame be the driving factor in your decisions; let the love of God and the desire to please Him be your driver, and only then will you live a life of fulfilment and purpose, and be all that you are.

You Are the Solution

Exodus 3:9-12, New Living translation

Look! The cry of the people of Israel has reached me, and I have seen how harshly the Egyptians abuse them. Now go, for I am sending you to Pharaoh. You must lead my people Israel out of Egypt. But Moses protested to God, 'Who am I to appear before Pharaoh? Who am I to lead the people of Israel out of Egypt?' God answered, 'I will be with you . . .'

Like Moses, many of us are too concerned with what we perceive as weaknesses or limitations in a certain area rather than focussing on what God has instructed us to do. God's people, the Israelites, were being oppressed in Egypt, and God had a plan to free them from their suffering. His plan was Moses. Moses, however, refused. He didn't want to go because he did not feel qualified. Notice that when Moses questioned God's choice of him; God didn't join him and begin to list what qualities made him suitable and unsuitable; He simply replied, 'I will be with you'. That's all you need to know. In your every endeavour, when God calls you to do something beyond your ability, all that matters is that God is with you!

When you walk with God, you have to know what questions are important and those that are of no consequence. God had chosen Moses for a specific task. He wasn't interested in Moses' past mistakes, his qualifications, or lack thereof; all He wanted to know was 'was he available?' It's the same question He's asking you: Are you available? The answer to the world's problems lies with us as Christians. Jesus's ministry was and still is all about people. Jesus isn't concerned with you advancing up the corporate ladder (not that these things are wrong); He is more concerned with the number of lives you touch as you climb the ladder. Lives are literally depending on you to step out into what God has called you to do. If Moses had not obeyed God, the Israelites may have died at Pharaoh's hands.

For many unbelievers, a common reason given for not believing in God is the evident suffering in the world. A popular question asked is 'if God exists, why there is so much suffering in the world?' I am going to be slightly controversial and say, the issue is not God; the issue is with us, His people. People are suffering and being oppressed before our very eyes because the children of God refuse to take their place as enforcers of God's will on this earth. God created man to accomplish His purposes on earth, and this is demonstrated in Genesis 1:28 when God blessed man and gave him the edict to go forth, occupy the earth, and have dominion (or govern) the earth. The children of God have not taken dominion; we have not taken our rightful place, and until we do, some things won't change. It is not enough to pray for change; we are the change we seek!

Show Me the Way!

Proverbs 3:5-6, New Living Translation

Trust in the Lord with all your heart; do not depend on your own understanding. Seek His will in all you do and He will show you which path to take.

One particular day, I was watching a movie and was reminded of the end credits of a martial arts movie, which struck a chord within me. It said and I quote, 'Only those on journeys will be shown the dim roads that lead the way home'.

As believers, we are on a journey. There is a destination, and for us home is eternity with Christ. Many a time this journey is arduous and fraught with twists and turns. Sometimes the road we are travelling on is dark and menacing with many unknowns, but that is not God's intention. God desires that we know His will, as He constantly speaks to us every day. We are instructed to be confident in the Lord and acknowledge Him as the all-knowing One, and He will illuminate our paths. He alone is the One who can make those crooked paths straight and cause light to shine on those areas of our lives that are darkened with confusion and doubt.

You are on an exciting journey where the Word of God will be tried and tested daily, but if you abide in the Lord and make Him your dwelling place, He will lead you home. Isaiah 42:16, NKJV, says, 'I will bring the blind by a way they did not know; I will lead them in paths they have not known. I will make darkness light before them, and crooked places straight. These things I will do for them, and not forsake them'.

You have already taken the first step of the journey; you have accepted Christ as the Lord of your life and believe that He died for your sins (and if you haven't made that decision, I encourage you to make that decision today). Sadly, many Christians don't finish the journey with joy because they let their situations dictate their attitude. Your journey has a conclusion, but it also has a purpose. Christ's journey was to conclude at the cross of Calvary for the purpose of saving humanity from the penalty of sin and birthing generations of followers who would continue His work on earth. There you have the end of the matter, but you also have purpose. The journey to the cross was neither pleasant nor was it easy; Christ endured all manner of suffering for our sakes. He was whipped mercilessly, mocked, spat on and despised, but at the end He could say, 'It is finished!' (John 19:30)

Brethren, it is a finished work! Look for the purpose in your pain, the testimony in your test, and the sermon in your struggle. Let the Spirit of God lead you in all things as you prepare for home. What you do in this life will determine what you will do for eternity. Make your life count! We are all on a journey specific to our God-ordained purpose; so when things get tough, and they will, don't quit because as the Chinese proverb says, 'only those on journeys will be shown the dim roads that lead the way home'.

What Have You Done for Others Lately?

Isaiah 61:1-2, New Living Translation

'The Spirit of the Sovereign Lord is upon me, for the Lord has anointed me to bring good news to the poor. He has sent me to comfort the broken-hearted and to proclaim that captives will be release and prisoners will be freed. He has sent me to tell those who mourn that the time of the Lord's favour has come . . .'

This is one of my favourite scriptures as it challenges me to move beyond my own needs and reminds me of why I am here. I call this scripture—'A Call to Action'. It summarises quite nicely the ministry of Jesus. While He was on earth, this was His passion and His purpose—He went about healing people, freeing them from situations that had held them bound. He forgave their sins, and in so doing released them from the mistakes of the past, but more importantly He shared with them the good news of salvation. You are called to do likewise. 'For God called you to do good even if it means suffering, just as Christ suffered for you. He is your example and you must follow in His steps' (1 Pet. 2:21, NLT).

It's not enough to say that you are a follower of Christ, what exactly are you following? 1 John 2:6, NLT, says,'Those who say they live in God should live their lives as Jesus did.' The Bible also says in the book of James, 'Faith without works is useless' (James 2:20, NLT). How do you demonstrate the faith that you have in Christ? When people meet you, can they immediately see that there is something different about you or do they faint from shock when told you are a Christian? Do you leave people better or bitter? Do people feel the brightness of your presence when you enter a room or do they feel like what little light was present has now been snuffed out by your arrival?

Life is fleeting. We go to bed each night and just assume that we will wake up the next day. We make plans for tomorrow, next month and next year, taking for granted that we will still be alive. Life was never meant to be about the accumulation of material things which decay, but the pursuit of things that last forever. Matthew 6:33, CEV, says, 'But more than anything else, put God's work first and do what He wants. Then the other things will be yours as well.'

If you are struggling to find your purpose in life, start by helping others. Be a blessing to those around you, volunteer at a homeless shelter, mentor a young child, provide a listening ear to a colleague in trouble, and so on. There are so many hurting people around you. When Jesus encountered people that were in need, He demonstrated His faith in God by responding with acts of love. So instead of going to God day after day with a shopping list of personal requests, switch your attention to those around you. Ask God to open your eyes to the pain of others and give you the opportunity to bring healing, comfort, and love. Finding purpose is not as hard as you think. As you go about doing what Jesus did, He will make His purpose for your life known, and it is then that you will find the true meaning of life and genuine fulfilment.

The Plan Still Stands!

Luke 22:31-32, King James Version

And the Lord said, Simon, Simon, behold, Satan hath desired to have you, that he may sift you as wheat: but I have prayed for thee, that thy faith fail not: and when thou art converted, strengthen thy brethren.

The Contemporary English Version puts it like this: 'Simon, listen to me! Satan has demanded the right to test each one of you, as a farmer does when he separates wheat from the husks. But Simon, I have prayed that your faith will be strong. And when you have come back to me, help the others.'

While reading this passage, my attention was drawn to the last line, which says, 'and *when* thou art converted . . .' This caught my attention because there was no question in Jesus's mind as to whether Peter would be converted. He didn't say 'if ' or 'should' you be converted, He was very clear—'when' you are converted. I checked up the meaning of the word 'converted' in *Vine's Dictionary*, and it means 'turning away' in the case of repentance; or 'turning to' in the case of faith. In other words, Christ was telling Peter, I have prayed for you that your faith will not fail, and when you have repented and returned to the faith, strengthen others around you who are also struggling (paraphrased). Trials are not just to be endured or overcome; your breakthrough is meant to encourage others and give them strength to get through their own struggles. You have gone through certain things so that you can encourage others in similar circumstances.

God had a plan for Peter's life. He wasn't ignorant of the mistakes Peter had made in the past and was well aware of those he would make in the future. However, none of this changed God's plans or intentions towards Peter. Oftentimes, we get so weighed down with the challenges and disappointments we face in life, forgetting that the One who wrote the story knows how the story ends. You win!' It's in Christ that we find out who we are and what we are living for. Long before we first heard of Christ and got our hopes up, He had

His eye on us, had designs on us for glorious living, part of the overall purpose He is working out in everything and everyone' (Eph. 1:11-12, MSG).

We need to stop making life-changing decisions based on temporary circumstances and look at situations with the eyes of the spirit (from God's standpoint based on His Word) rather than how we feel and what we can physically see. There are so many people all over the world who have used their challenges as a platform of hope and restoration for others and are changing lives.

It's time to leave the past in the past and return to your faith. God has a plan and He's waiting for you.

When Struggling with
Low Self-Esteem . . .

'So God created human beings in his own image; in the image
of God he created them; male and female he created them. So
God created human being in his own image. In the image of
God he created them male and female he created them.'
(Gen. 1:27)

Intricately Woven, Fearfully Made!

Psalm 139:13-17, Contemporary English Version

You are the one who put me together inside my mother's body, and I praise you because of the wonderful way you created me. Everything you do is marvellous! Of this I have no doubt. Nothing about me is hidden from you! I was secretly woven together deep in the earth below, but with your own eyes you saw my body being formed. Even before I were born, you had written in your book everything I would do. Your thoughts are far beyond my understanding, much more than I could ever imagine.

The above scripture illustrates the amount of love and attention that went into creating you. You're not a blip on the radar or a product of chance; God created you intentionally and with great precision, down to the very last detail. The Bible says, 'And the very hairs on your head are all numbered' (Matt. 10:30 NLT).

When the Bible says you are 'fearfully made', it means God created you in reverence; He took his time in creating you and left nothing to chance. God is passionate about you and took great care in creating you. Your pain and your hurts matter to God. He cares about your well being, even the little seemingly insignificant moments in your life matter to Him. God says in Isaiah 49:15-16 (paraphrased), He cannot forget you because your name is inscribed on the palms of His hands. God took great care and attention in creating you because you are important to Him.

Stop looking downwards; look up! Hold your head high. You are somebody and you matter. You may have believed the lies of friends, family, teachers, and so many others that didn't know any better, but it's time to put an end to that chapter of your life. You are not worthless, you are not rubbish and you are not unlovable! You need to walk in the truth of who you are and God's love for you. Man cannot determine how far you go. Don't let people place a value on you because you are invaluable. Don't let people place boundaries on how far you can go and what you can achieve because you can do all things through Christ who strengthens you (Phil. 4:13). It is the manufacturer of an object that determines it use.

There will be moments in your life when you will feel discouraged, lonely, and unwanted, questioning yourself and your abilities, but it is in those times that you need to encourage yourself. The psalmist said, 'I will lift up my eyes to the hills—From whence comes my help? My help comes from the LORD, Who made heaven and earth' (Ps. 121:1-2 NKJV). Your life cannot be worthless or meaningless unless you allow it to be. You are not an accident or a mistake; God has a plan for you. You are not the mistakes you made, but you are simply one who forgot who they are and went the wrong way momentarily. It's time to live like one who has a purpose and the purpose of your existence is found in the One who created you. There is nothing you have done, could do or will do that will separate you from God's love for you. It is eternal.

Make a conscious decision today to refute all negative thinking and anything or anyone who tries to devalue you. When thoughts arise, which make you doubt or question yourself, renew your mind with what God says about you in Psalm 139.

The Potter's Touch

Isaiah 64:8, New International Version

Yet you, Lord, are our Father. We are the clay, you are the Potter; we all are the work of your hand.

While reading the novel *A Heart of Devotion*[2] by Tia McCollors, I was reminded of the way God works with us. There is a scene in the book where two friends visit a pottery shop, and the instructor gives them advice on how to mould the clay—'The clay is totally in your hands. It has no choice but to conform to however you shape it. Gentle moulding works, but sometimes you have to apply a little pressure to get the shape you want ... If the clay gets too dry, it will become resistant to moulding, so you have to add a little to water it ... After you've finished, you coat it with a glaze that acts like a seal to give the pottery texture and brilliance. Then you put the finished pieces in the fire.' This represents God's relationship with us.

The shape of the clay is governed by the direction of the potter; whatsoever the potter desires that is what the clay becomes. Some of the difficult experiences we face in life are because we are going through a process of reshaping, and more pressure is required to remould our character and change the way we respond to certain situations. For example, it may be that you are still too sensitive to what people say about you or still too quick to get angry. At other times, like clay, we become stagnant and dry and need the water of His Word to revitalise us.

My favourite part of the pottery process is what happens before the clay is passed through the fire. The clay is 'coated with a glaze that acts like a seal to give the pottery texture and brilliance'. This is a beautiful analogy of God's covering over your life. He pours all His love into creating and moulding you and then when He has finished, He covers you with Himself, which adds depth (of character) and brilliance (supernatural ability) to your natural talent. That is why you can never be ordinary because God's power is at work in your life. You have His creativity, His ability to plan and deliver, His business savvy, His patience, His love and so on. All that God is you are, for you were created in His image!

God is shaping your life and your destiny. When a potter moulds clay, it is a delicate process and not something that can be rushed. Don't compare yourself or where you are now with that of others. The beauty of clay is that every piece is unique; no two pieces are ever or can ever be the same, and one thing is for sure—we are all being shaped differently and for a different purpose.

God is the Potter and you are the clay. When He created you, He had a plan in mind. He knew where you would fit best, and daily, you are being shaped as He moulds you into the man or the woman He created you to be. Know that fiery trials and temptations will come but rest assured, whenever you miss it or when the pressure is almost too much to bear, the 'Potter' has got you covered and is always on hand to mould you back into shape.

The Choice Is Yours, Choose Wisely!

Jeremiah 1:5, The Message

'Before I shaped you in the womb, I knew all about you. Before you saw the light of day, I had holy plans for you . . .'

Sometimes when God places in our hearts the desire to do something and it doesn't materialise straight away, we question whether we heard Him in the first place. Other times we dismiss the idea as completely too far-fetched to be real. You are right; anything God wants you to do will always be beyond your abilities and it will always dwell in the realms of impossibility, but that's where God delights to show himself. He adds His 'super' to your natural ability and gives you the 'supernatural' ability to do what for others is impossible.

Everything has a time and a season. Consider the birth of a child. It doesn't happen overnight; there is a gestation period in which the child develops all of its vital organs and everything it needs to survive in the world. When a baby comes too early, it is deemed premature. It has arrived before its maturity period. It's the same way with our dreams and our goals. There is always a period of preparation before birth!

If your desire to start that business, change careers, or even start that course won't go away, rest assured that God has placed that seed inside of you and He will always provide for the vision ('provision'). You must push ahead in the face of opposition. Don't be afraid to be different. Don't try and fit in with the crowd, don't try and be like anyone other than yourself. The world will tell you that it can't be done; that it's not possible, that's, it never been done before; that you don't have the right qualifications, the right accent, the right postcode, and so on and so forth! But when the world says *no*, your response must be an emphatic *yes!* 'Christ gives you the strength to face anything' (Phil. 4:13, CEV).

So refuse to quit. You may not be where you want to be, but you are definitely not where you used to be! Look for the positive in every experience;

choose to see the silver lining in every dark cloud. Opposition will always precede success. Stop looking downwards and lift your head up high. You are the deciding factor in your destiny—you can either press forward with God, in the face of negativity and difficulty, or give up and never experience the joy of fulfilling your dreams. The choice, as they say, is yours!

When You Need Direction . . .

'Ask me and I will tell you remarkable secrets you
do not know about things to come.'
(Jer. 33:3)

If You Only Knew

1 Corinthians 2:9-12, New Living Translation

No eye has seen, no ear has heard, and no mind has imagined what God has prepared for those who love him. But it was to us that God revealed these things by his Spirit. For his Spirit searches out everything and shows us God's deep secrets. No one can know a person's thoughts except that person's own spirit and no one can know God's thoughts except God's own Spirit. And we have received God's Spirit (not the world's spirit), so we can know the wonderful things God has freely given us.

For many of us, our challenges would be so much easier to bear if we knew how things would turn out and what would happen after we had taken a step as a result of a major decision. However, we don't know the future and that is why we have to call on God for direction. I don't know about you, but there was a time when I thought that getting direction from God or discerning His will was like trying to find the proverbial needle in a haystack! However, one particular morning, I had a light bulb moment . . . Now it's not that I didn't know this already, but sometimes you know things in your head that haven't quite settled in your heart.

All of mankind is searching for where they fit in this world and what they are supposed to be doing with their lives. Some people think the answer can be found on a mountain in Nepal or Tibet whilst others believe the pursuit of wealth or intellectual trophies holds the key. Sadly, none of these will satisfy. Even as Christians we sometimes find ourselves doing the same things those without faith do in a bid to find the 'meaning of our existence.'

For the longest time, my prayer has been 'God, why am I here?' to the point where if it were possible for God to get fed up with me, He would have said, 'For My sake, girl, change the record', but God is patient. In this scripture, God showed me that all the answers I desire are already on the inside of me. You can know God's will for your life; it's not meant to be a secret. The Holy

Spirit was given to you that you might know that which is already yours, the things that have been given to you by grace. The things that God has in in store for you are beyond your imagination. I love the Message translation of this scripture, which says, 'No one's ever seen or heard anything like this, never so much as imagined anything quite like it—What God has arranged for those who love Him but you've seen and heard it because God by His Spirit has brought it all out into the open before you. The Spirit, not content to flit around on the surface, dives into the depths of God, and brings out what God planned all along. Who knows what you're thinking and planning except you yourself? The same with God—except that He not only knows what He's thinking, but He lets us in on it. God offers a full report on the gifts of life and salvation that He is giving us.'

It is not God's intention that you should be ignorant of the things He is doing. His desire is that you know His plans. If you want to know what you should be doing now, listen to His Spirit on the inside of you as He directs you, knowing that whatever He asks you to do or reveals to you will always require faith.

Your Will Be Done

Matthew 13:11, Amplified Bible

And He replied to them, 'to you it has been given to know the secrets and mysteries of the Kingdom of heaven . . .'

I find it very interesting how you can read a particular chapter in the Bible or a particular verse several times and then one moment 'see it' for the first time. One particular morning, I happened to be reading the book of Matthew and came across the parable of the sower, a story we are all very familiar with. What drew my attention were not the different types of people who received the Word (important as this is to know) but the conversation that ensued between Jesus and His disciples after the parable was told. The disciples wanted to know why Jesus was speaking to the people in parables and His response was that the people had to be taught in parables, as they would not understand if Jesus spoke to them plainly.

Similarly, it has been given to you to know the will of God. Oftentimes, we pray saying, if it is your will, let it be done. This sentence (in my opinion) carries with it doubt, for you are basically saying you don't know what God's will or desire is in that particular situation, so you are hedging your bets hoping for a favourable outcome. However, the above scripture clearly illustrates that we do know the will of God. You have His Word written in the Bible and His very Spirit and presence on the inside of you. The Bible says in John 16:13, NKJV, 'However, when He, the Spirit of truth, has come, He will guide you into all truth; for He will not speak on His own authority, but whatever He hears He will speak and He will tell you things to come.'

The precepts of the Christian life are meant to be complicated, but I do believe as human beings we complicate simple matters. The reason why we struggle sometimes to enter into God's best is because we don't know our rights or heritage. The Message translation of the Bible says in Hosea 4:6, 'My people are ruined because they don't know what's right or true'. You need to know what is rightfully yours so that you can prayerfully receive it.

I don't believe God intended us to go through life by trial and error, or make decisions on a whim. His intention is that we know which job to take, which house to buy, where to invest, which relationships to pursue and those to avoid, and so on. So each time you come to a crossroad in life or have a decision to make, take a moment to thank God for wisdom and insight which He has placed on the inside of you. Then, weigh up your options in line with His Word, trusting Him to lead and direct your steps, confident in the knowledge that His will shall surely be done.

Father Knows Best!

Psalm 118:8, New King James Version

It is better to trust and take refuge in the Lord than to put confidence in man.

'Trust me!' Only two words, but two words that people find really hard to do, whether it's in relation to God or to people. When people we know and see say these words, it is often received with scepticism, much less when spoken by a God that we do not know and we cannot see! Past experience and disappointments have made it easier for us to make decisions based on what we can see with our natural eyes, but God is calling us to a deeper relationship with Him. Trust is a big issue for many people because of their past experiences, but it is necessary in order to experience the abundant life Christ died to give us.

For those of you like me who are analytical and logical by nature, our natural inclination is to ask questions to make sense of life's anomalies and our expectation is that one plus one equals two. We don't like unanswered questions, but God uses this to train us in trust. Oftentimes, we try to use human wisdom and reasoning to explain spiritual things, but 'the things of God cannot be explained, only revealed'. God wants us to leave our plans, hopes, dreams, and problems in His hands, and that can be difficult if you are a make-it-happen kind of person. God doesn't work to our timetable; He is the author of time and has His own!

When told that they were going to the Promised Land, the Israelites were filled with excitement. They were finally leaving the place of oppression and depression at the hands of the Egyptians for a place of dominion and elevation. However, on the way to the Promised Land they passed through the wilderness, where they encountered trials and began to complain, questioning Moses's leadership. We read this story and marvel at how the Israelites could have doubted God after the miracles He performed, such as the parting of the Red Sea to save them from the Egyptians who were chasing them.

However, here we are in the 21st Century and things are not that different. We have experienced the grace of God personally as well as indirectly via the testimonies of others, yet when we need direction or are faced with problems, we, like the Egyptians, focus on the size of the problem rather than the size of our God!

Don't let the fear of the unknown or the presence of challenges stop you from entering into your Promised Land. Your Promised Land might be writing a book, starting a business, launching an album, or writing your first play. Whatever it is, know that God is the One ordering your steps and He is interested in every detail of your life (Ps. 37:23, NLT).

Speak Life

Proverbs 18:20-21, The Message

Words satisfy the mind as much as fruit does the stomach; good talk is as gratifying as a good harvest. Words kill, words give life; they're either poison or fruit—you choose.

This scripture is so powerful, yet powerfully underestimated! The Bible is clear that what you say determines the direction of your life. When we are going through difficult periods in our lives or things don't go the way we expect, human tendency is to complain and talk negatively, thereby reinforcing the very situation we desire to come out off. If you consistently speak your predicament, then where will the change come from? When Jesus was tempted by the devil (Matt. 4:1-11; Luke 4:1-13), He didn't say 'I am in the wilderness' or 'I am hungry'. He consistently responded to each temptation with what was written in the Word of God. You need to do the same. Stating the obvious doesn't do any good; it only causes you to focus on the problem rather than seeking a solution.

The Word of God is your compass. If you are not sure what to do and you need direction, the answers can be found in His Word. The Bible says in Psalm 119:105 NLT, 'Your word is a lamp to guide my feet and a light for my path.' God through the power of His Words created the world and through that same power upholds the earth. The world was dark and void, so God said, 'Let there be light', and there was light (Gen. 1:3). He spoke into existence His desire. Faith-filled words release the creative power of God and bring about supernatural changes in your life, but conversely, negative words (which are based on fear) bring about destruction and keep you rooted in your problem.

Jesus while talking with His disciples said, 'For assuredly, I say to you, whoever says to this mountain, "Be removed and be cast into the sea," and does not doubt in his heart, but believes that those things he says will be done, he will have whatever he says' (Mark 11:23, NKJV). Jesus was explaining to the disciples the principles and power of faith, which are: if you believe and do not doubt, you will have whatever you say. I think this works both ways. If you believe in something enough (whether positive or negative), you will have what you say!

Some of the things in your life today are a product of the things you said yesterday. You don't have bad luck and bad things don't always happen to you. Life is comprised of ups and downs; no one is exempt. The people who overcome are those who choose to see beyond their present to what their future can be. When you need guidance, God promised He will instruct you and teach you in the way you should go (Ps. 32:8, NIV). If you want to change the direction of your life, change what you say. Words are spiritual currency, so be careful how you spend.

In Times of Need . . .

'I have strength for all things in Christ who empowers me [I am
ready for anything and equal to anything through Him Who infuses
inner strength into me; I am self-sufficient in Christ's sufficiency].'
(Phil. 4:13)

The Lord Is Your Shepherd

Psalm 23, New Living Translation

The Lord is my shepherd; I have all that I need.
He lets me rest in green meadows; he leads me beside peaceful streams.
He renews my strength. He guides me along right paths, bringing honour to his
*   name. Even when I walk through the darkest valley,*
I will not be afraid, for you are close beside me. Your rod and your staff protect
*   and comfort me.*
You prepare a feast for me in the presence of my enemies.
You honour me by anointing my head with oil. My cup overflows with blessings. Surely
*   your goodness and unfailing love will pursue me all the days of my life, and*
I will live in the house of the Lord forever.

I've read this scripture so many times and pretty much know it from memory, but one particular day while meditating on it I gained a fresh understanding of its meaning.

The Lord is your Shepherd, the One that takes care of you and the One that leads you when you don't know where you are going. He even leads you in those situations where you think He is absent. When the needs are more than the means, He is Jehovah-Jireh, the Lord your Provider, the one who supplies all your needs. When the tears are more than the laughter, He is your Comforter. Paul in his second letter to the Corinthian church said, 'All praise to God, the Father of our Lord Jesus Christ. God is our merciful Father and the source of all comfort' (2 Cor. 2:3, NLT). If you are feeling the loss of a loved one or your heart is overwhelmed with the pain of rejection and you feel like the hurt will never end, you will find comfort in Him. In the midst of confusion, He is Jehovah-Shalom, your Peace. For every situation you will ever face in life, He is the solution!

On that wonderful morning, as I sat on the train to work, verses four and six of Psalm 23 cried out to me. They spoke to the part of me that yearns for an end to the struggles. In those verses, God told me that fear and death have no hold over me. God said even when you face death (or what looks like death), 'I am with you!' You have no reason to be afraid or worried because 'He is your refuge and strength, always ready to help in times of trouble' (Ps. 46:1, NLT). Another translation of the Bible calls Him your fortress (a heavily protected and impenetrable building, a shield of defence). What a beautiful analogy. This is who God is to you!

A shepherd cares for his sheep and will protect them at all costs. Tell me what can separate you from that kind of love? Can sickness? Can money? Can death? Can age? Whatever you're going through, whatever you need, the Lord is your Shepherd. His faithfulness and mercies are new every morning, which is why you have not been consumed by your problems.

You Are in Safe Hands

Isaiah 49:16, New Living Translation

'See, I have written your name on the palms of My hands . . .'

One day, while driving home from work I was listening to a song titled 'Safe in His Hands' from the album *Declaring His Love* by Muyiwa and Riversongz. The lyrics to the song reminded me of God's unchanging love for us. The track starts off with Muyiwa talking about his family background and how he lost his parents at a very young age—so they never got the opportunity to see him grow up to be the man he is today. He talks about how things have changed, friends and loved ones he has lost along the way. However, the thing that struck me most whilst listening to the song was that despite the loss he had experienced and the loneliness he sometimes felt, he was reassured of God's love and His presence.

Maintaining a firm belief in God's presence even in times of trouble is a challenge for some of us. We think (subconsciously) that Christianity equates to insulation from life's negative experiences, but this is so far from the truth. Trouble does not distinguish or show favouritism; it is impartial to colour, sex, age and creed. This is where so many of us get it wrong. We think belief in God shields us from life experiences; well, it doesn't. The important thing to understand and recognise is that the presence of problems does not indicate an absence of God. He is 'always ready to help in times of trouble' (Ps. 46:1, NLT).

This song really ministered to me because it made me acknowledge that during life's storms, though we are buffeted from side to side, we are not destroyed because He is holding us tightly and securely in His hands. God is not moved by economic uncertainty, rising interest rates, or inflated petrol prices. Earthquakes, tsunamis, tornados, or global warming do not intimidate or shake Him. There are no guarantees in life, but one thing you can be sure of is that in the midst of life's challenges, God is the one thing that will never change!

I leave you with these two verses from Psalm 56:3-4 (paraphrased)—
'Whenever you are afraid, put your trust in Him. Bless the name of the Lord
for He is true to His word and the promises He has made to you. If you have
really put your trust in God, why are you still worried or anxious? With God's
hands wrapped securely around you what can mere mortals do to you?' So
wipe your tears away and put your hope in God!

Don't Worry, It's All Taken Care Of

Luke 12:22-26, New Living Translation

Then, turning to his disciples, Jesus said, 'That is why I tell you not to worry about everyday life—whether you have enough food to eat or enough clothes to wear. For life is more than food, and your body more than clothing. Look at the ravens. They don't plant or harvest or store food in barns, for God feeds them. And you are far more valuable to him than any birds! Can all your worries add a single moment to your life? And if worry can't accomplish a little thing like that, what's the use of worrying over bigger things?'

Given the current economic climate, natural disasters and premature loss of life, people are worried. They are worried about how the bills will be paid whilst struggling to keep a roof over the heads of them and their families. Jobs that once represented long-term security for the masses have been added to the list of casualties from the economic downturn and can no longer be guaranteed. Every day you switch on the television or open the paper with breaking news about the latest calamity to befall your nation and/or other nations.

So what do you do in the face of such depressing and unsavoury news? How do you prevent yourself from flying into a state of panic at the unsettling events around you? The Bible gives us the blueprint for living in these tumultuous and trying days—'Don't worry about anything, but pray about everything; with thankful hearts offer up your prayers and requests to God. Then, because you belong to Christ Jesus, God will bless you with peace that no one can completely understand. And this peace will control the way you think and feel' (Phil. 4:6-7, CEV).

Worrying changes nothing! It doesn't add to your life in any way, but rather the complete opposite. It takes away from you by destroying your health and your relationships. Instead of spending sleepless nights worrying about the things you cannot change, cast your cares on God because He cares for you (1 Pet. 5:7, CEV). Jesus was trying to show the disciples how ineffective worrying is by comparing their needs with those of the birds, and if you read further on in the chapter, the flowers in the field. Ravens like humans require sustenance, but somehow, without planting seeds or storing food in barns, they still manage to eat each day and survive. If God can take care of the birds, why do you think He won't take care of you? You are of more value to Him than the birds in the air and the flowers in the fields!

Worrying stems from a place of fear and is an expression of doubt in God's ability to provide for and take care of you. Fear doesn't come from God. The key to remaining unshaken in these times of instability is to focus on the one that does not change, taking your requests to Him in prayer. Approach Him with a heart of thanksgiving and faith in His ability to meet your needs. In times of need, instead of worrying, 'Give your burdens to the Lord and He will take care of you. He will not permit the godly to slip and fall' (Ps. 55:22, NLT).

Waiting on God . . .

'At the time I have decided, my words will come true.
You can trust what I say about the future. It may take a
long time, but keep on waiting—it will happen!'
(Hab. 2:3)

When Lord, When?

Psalm 40:1, New King James Version

I waited patiently and expectantly for the Lord; and He inclined to me and heard my cry.

Waiting on God is one of the hardest things to do. It's bad enough waiting in a queue in the supermarket or waiting for a bus that should have turned up thirty minutes ago. Surely with God, it must be different? I mean He is God. He could do it before I've even thought about it! Furthermore, the Bible says 'Ask and it shall be given to you . . .' (Matt. 7:7), so you ask and no response. Maybe you are chasing too much of the things, so instead you passionately pursue the things of God; after all, if you 'delight yourself in the Lord, He shall give you the desires of your heart' (Ps. 37:4), but still no sign of Him. What are you doing wrong? The answer in most cases is nothing!

Sometimes God doesn't answer our prayers immediately for the following reasons: to get your attention off what you desire and back on Him; the timing is not right; to stretch your faith; the circumstances are not right; to remind you that He's in control or because there is sin which is hindering you. Sometimes it has nothing to do with God and everything to do with the fact that you haven't obeyed the last instruction He gave you. Whatever the reason, waiting is uncomfortable, but sometimes needful.

Waiting for the manifestation of a promise brings you to a place of maturity by birthing patience in you. James wrote 'But let patience have its perfect work, that you may be perfect and complete, lacking nothing' (James 1:4, NKJV). Other times, if your desires involve someone else, it's about God changing their mind about certain things and opening their eyes to what's in front of them. If you think about the solar system, certain things have to come into alignment before a full moon can occur. It's much the same in our lives. Certain events and people must be aligned for us to reap the full benefits of God's blessings. When we refuse to wait, and jump ahead of God's timing, we short-change ourselves of the full blessing and in some cases, sacrifice God's best for average.

Waiting on God is not a choice, but rather a necessity if ultimately you want God's best. Don't try and work things out yourself or manipulate circumstances in your favour—this will only lead to further delay and potentially hurt and pain for others as well as yourself. Waiting on God is hard, but a life built on trust in Him is a life that learns to wait patiently and expectantly knowing that when God does show up, He will do exceeding, abundantly above all you could ask or think! (Eph. 3:20)

'When it looks like nothing is happening, God is working!'—Taken from Charles Stanley's *The Grace to Wait.*

Why Wait?

Isaiah 40:31, Amplified Bible

But those who wait for the Lord [who expect, look for, and hope in Him] shall change and renew their strength and power; they shall lift their wings and mount up [close to God] as eagles [mount up to the sun]; they shall run and not be weary, they shall walk and not faint or become tired!

Society today is such that the solution to any problem can be found at the click of a button. Technology has made it such that people don't want to wait for anything any more. Waiting builds your character by teaching you to be patient, but patience is fast becoming a 'nice to have' and instant gratification par for the course. Whilst uncomfortable, patience is essential to the successful growth and life of a Christian. The book of Hebrews says, 'Patient endurance is what you need now, so that you will continue to do God's will. Then you will receive all that He has promised' (Heb. 10:36, NLT).

In times past, when conversing with a 'pen pal' or relative who lived in another country, you would write letters and wait several weeks and sometimes months before receiving a reply. Today, we have email, Skype, Facebook, and a host of other social media for getting in touch with people immediately. The likes of instant messaging have made staying in touch easier and people more accessible. Gone are the days of waiting. Sadly, this desire for instant gratification has crept unknowingly and rather insidiously into the church. The ability to wait patiently is a trait not easily found, sadly even amongst some Christians.

God works with us as individuals and in different ways, but one experience shared by all Christians is the 'waiting experience'. This waiting could be for a husband, a child, a new job, or that first business contract. Whatever it is, most of us have been waiting some length of time for a breakthrough in a certain area of our lives. Waiting is not a pleasurable experience and we have become so weary with the process, but that shouldn't be the case. God's

Word says that 'when we wait on Him we find renewed strength; we keep on moving and do not grow weary; we won't faint or grow tired; we will not give up!' (paraphrased) When we truly wait on God in faith, we are strengthened and empowered by His Word, knowing that the fulfilment of His promises will come to pass. You only grow weary in waiting when you stop believing. If you are convinced of the promise, you will wait with eager, anticipation, and expectation, knowing that the fulfilment of the promise is near.

What are you are waiting for? Have you become tired of waiting and pretty much given up or do you approach each day with excitement, wondering whether this will be the day when your change comes? It doesn't matter how long you have waited or how old you are. Jesus in talking to His disciples said, 'The sky and the earth will not last forever, but my words will' (Mark 13:31, CEV). Don't stop believing; God is faithful, and His Word cannot return to Him void (empty, ineffective and useless), without accomplishing the thing it set out to do.

There Is Power in His Word

Isaiah 55:10-11, Contemporary English Version

'Rain and snow fall from the sky. But they don't return without watering the earth that produces seeds to plant and grain to eat. That's how it is with my words. They don't return to me without doing everything I send them to do.'

God likens His Word to the rain and snow that come down from heaven and cannot return to heaven but water the earth, making it bud and grow. In so doing they provide seed for the farmer to sow and crop for the one that needs to eat. In the same way, once His Word goes forth or is spoken, it cannot remain dormant or return to Him without having fulfilled the needs of those for who it was sent. Furthermore, not only shall His Word accomplish that which He planned but it shall also bring forth fruit and multiply in your life. This is in line with the very first instruction that God gave man at creation when He said, 'Be fruitful and multiply, fill the earth!' (Gen. 1:28, NLT)

In other words, if it is possible for rain to fall and the ground to remain dry (and we all know that it is impossible), then God's Word can fail. We need to recognise that what we think is irrelevant, God will do what He said He is going to do; when He said He was going to do it and for the very reason He said it. It doesn't matter how long you have waited for things to change, God's Word is true! Once His Word has been spoken, by virtue of the fact that God cannot lie, it must come to pass. God's Word transcends time; His Word transcends you! Abraham waited twenty-five years for the birth of his son Isaac, but it came to pass; Joseph went through the pit and the prison before he got to the palace, but God's Word still came to pass and he was made the Prime Minister! Mary and Martha saw their brother die and waited four days before Jesus arrived, spoke a Word and Lazarus was raised from the dead!

During the period of waiting, especially when you have waited so long, there is a temptation to give up, but it is in those times especially that you need to stand firm and give thanks, for the fulfilment of His Word is near. His Word is not limited by time or circumstance. When you speak God's Word, you are declaring His promises, plans, and purposes over your life, and everything in your life must eventually align to that Word. So hold on a little while longer, and don't give up. You are closer than when you first believed!

Battling with Insecurities . . .

'. . . For My strength and power are made perfect (fulfilled and completed)
and show themselves most effective in [your] weakness.'
(2 Cor. 12:9)

Thank God for Weaknesses

1 Corinthians 1:25-29, New Living Translation

This foolish plan of God is wiser than the wisest of human plans, and God's weakness is stronger than the greatest of human strength. Remember, dear brothers and sisters, that few of you were wise in the world's eyes or powerful or wealthy when God called you. Instead, God chose things the world considers foolish in order to shame those who think they are wise. And he chose things that are powerless to shame those who are powerful. God chose things despised by the world; things counted as nothing at all, and used them to bring to nothing what the world considers important. As a result, no one can ever boast in the presence of God.

In today's society, it isn't cool to admit that you have a weakness. Those with weaknesses are deemed unsuitable, insignificant and somewhat inferior. However, with God the opposite is true. Having weaknesses makes you the perfect vessel for God's use! Our limitations are what drive us to our knees to seek His face.

According to the world's standards, where you are now and what you have accomplished does not make sense, but God has deliberately chosen to use the things this world considers foolish to confuse those who think they are wise. One version of the Bible uses the phrase 'confound the wise'. The word 'confound' means to 'leave speechless, to puzzle, to baffle or perplex, to mystify or bewilder'. Other definitions for 'confound' are 'defeat, thwart, and annihilate'. In other words (if I may paraphrase this Bible verse), when God uses you, He will thwart the plans of the seemingly wise (by the world's standards) and leave them in a state of utter confusion. The world may tell you, 'Not a chance', God says, 'Therefore I say to you, whatever things you ask when you pray, believe that you receive them and you will have them' (Mark 11:24, NKJV). Man says, 'You are not qualified', but God says, 'My grace is all you need; My power works best in weakness' (2 Cor. 12:9, NLT). People may say, 'You'll never make it', but God says, 'For I know the plans I have for you,' declares the Lord, 'plans to prosper you and not to harm you, plans to give you hope and a future' (Jer. 29:11, NIV).

You have become so preoccupied with your weaknesses and see them as hindrances to your success, failing to realise that they are the very things that God uses to demonstrate His power in your life. Stop focussing on what you don't have because whatever you give your attention will inevitably grow. The Bible is filled with great men and women of God who had weaknesses and by the world's standards were seen as unusable—unstable Peter, who was prone to impatience and anger; doubting Thomas, a man who had to see it before he would believe it. Matthew the tax collector; David the adulterer; the list is endless.

A jigsaw puzzle is comprised of many pieces. If any piece goes missing, the jigsaw is incomplete. You are an important piece to the creation puzzle. Stop worshipping your limitations and magnifying them above God—acknowledge them and hand them over to God, trusting Him to use them for you good and His glory!

Precious Treasures in Earthen Vessels

2 Corinthians 4:7, Amplified Bible

However, we possess this precious treasure [the divine Light of the Gospel] in [frail, human] vessels of earth that the grandeur and exceeding greatness of the power may be shown to be from God and not from ourselves.

Imagine a plant pot made of clay. Then imagine that pot containing a host of precious jewels such as gold and diamonds. You wouldn't expect to find such treasures in such a vessel—it would appear so out of place. In fact, if you were looking for precious stones, a pot of clay is the last place you would look. People may look at you and disregard you because of your appearance, experiences, or even past mistakes, but those are the very things God uses to fulfil His purpose here on earth.

You may be thinking 'I'm unlovable' or 'I don't fit the profile', but in God's eyes, the very things that you feel disqualify you are the very things that make you the perfect candidate. There are no 'lost causes' in the kingdom of God. God loves you, warts and all! Our human frailties are what make us chosen vessels for God's use. When you trust God to lead and direct you, He uses you to do the impossible so that His name is glorified. You are for a sign and wonder to those who refuse to believe. God is using your life to show forth His power so that others will desire to know Him.

God doesn't use the world's standards when choosing people He wants to use. He doesn't care how famous you are or how rich you are. He doesn't overlook the poor in favour of the rich or the weak in favour of the strong. The book of Job puts it like this: 'And God created us all; He has no favourites, whether rich or poor' (Job 34:19, CEV). He uses whom He chooses. He uses our human limitations to demonstrate the strength of His power, for it is in the times of our weaknesses that His strength is perfected.

Your imperfections are what make you perfect in God's eyes. Don't let others label or limit you. The world's criterion is perfection and ability; God desires a willing heart and availability.

Consider the Ants

Proverbs 30:24-28, New Living Translation

There are four things on earth that are small but unusually wise:

Ants—they aren't strong, but they store up food all summer.
Hyraxes—they aren't powerful, but they make their homes among the rocks.
Locusts—they have no king, but they march in formation.
Lizards—they are easy to catch, but they are found even in kings' palaces.

When you read this scripture, you discover that none of the excuses we give ourselves, others, or God hold water. Your colour, age, lack of qualifications, and so on, none of these things are valid reasons for you not being all that God has called you to be.

In this scripture we are told about some creatures that are small but 'unusually wise'. The New King James Version describes them as 'exceedingly wise'. The creatures in question are ants, rock badgers, locusts and lizards. The ants are not strong, yet they manage to store food throughout the summer. Locusts do not have a leader to keep them in line, yet they march in unity with none of them being out of place and with no one to lead or direct them. Lizards are easy to catch yet they are found in palaces.

These creatures do not allow their obvious physical limitations hold them back or intimidate them. If their size does not limit their capacity for operating wisely, then what's your excuse for why things are the way they are in your life? What's your excuse for having not progressed? What possible excuse could you have for not achieving more in your life? If a lizard can be found in the palace, why do you then think that you are destined to remain in the servants' quarters?

Lack of money, qualifications, or right of abode is not the issue; your issue is lack of wisdom. The Bible wonderfully illustrates the profit of wisdom saying, 'Through wisdom a house is built and by understanding it is established;

by knowledge the rooms are filled with all precious and pleasant riches' (Prov. 24:3, NKJV). Wisdom, understanding and knowledge all go hand in hand. At the time of creation, God blessed you and gave you dominion. This means that everything you need to succeed is already on the inside of you. So rather than looking at what you don't have or comparing yourself to others, start using the skills and gifts you do have.

Success is not determined by your skills but your ability to use the skills and gifts you have and turn challenges into opportunities, problems into solutions. All four small creatures in the main scripture mastered this technique through wisdom. You have no excuse; you are much bigger and far superior than all four creatures combined. It's time you stop making excuses and start living like one who has dominion.

Made in His Image

Genesis 1:26-28, Amplified Bible

God said, Let Us [Father, Son, and Holy Spirit] make mankind in Our image, after Our likeness, and let them have complete authority over the fish of the sea, the birds of the air, the [tame] beasts, and over all of the earth, and over everything that creeps upon the earth. So God created man in His own image, in the image and likeness of God He created him; male and female He created them. And God blessed them and said to them, be fruitful, multiply, and fill the earth, and subdue it [using all its vast resources in the service of God and man]; and have dominion over the fish of the sea, the birds of the air, and over every living creature that moves upon the earth.

I think we seriously underestimate the power of these words 'made in His image'. I know sometimes I do. The dictionary definition of an image is a 'picture that reproduces the likeness of some subject—usually a physical object or a person'. When God created you in His image, He gave you facets of His personality, such as creativity, intelligence, kindness, mercy, justice and perseverance. He created you so that you would be godlike on earth, exercising dominion in the earth and reproduce similar godlike offspring. That is, offspring that share your belief systems.

The biggest mistake you could ever make is to think that where you are now is where you will always be or that there is no purpose to your existence. Nobody ever creates anything without a purpose in mind much less the Creator of the universe! The Sony and Phillips of the audio and visual technology world didn't build TVs and hi-fi systems and then wonder what to use them for. They already had in mind what the problem was and then went about building products suitable for solving those problems. You are not a small fish in a big pond in God's eyes. You are not insignificant. You (yes, little old you!) are a solution to a problem. Think of a jigsaw puzzle; every single piece is important. Until all pieces fit together the puzzle is incomplete and doesn't make sense.

Insecurity comes from not knowing who you are. The Bible says in the book of Ephesians that you are God's workmanship, which means that time, effort and skill went into creating you—'For we are God's masterpiece. He has created us anew in Christ Jesus, so we can do the good things He planned for us long ago' (Eph. 2:10, NLT). If where you are right now does not demonstrate dominion, that is, is not a place of abundance, increase, prosperity, good health, and so on, then rest assured that where you are is temporary. Anything that does not glorify God will not be allowed to remain in your life unless you let it. If you want people to see you differently, you need to change the way you see yourself. See yourself as God sees you; fearfully and wonderfully crafted in His image!

Staying Anchored During Life's Storms . . .

'But you are a tower of refuge to the poor, O Lord, a
tower of refuge to the needy in distress. You are a refuge
from the storm and a shelter from the heat . . .'
(Isa. 25:4)

Holding On!

Psalm 33:11, New Living Translation

But the Lord's plans stand firm forever; his intentions can never be shaken.

I was reading a devotional one morning, and it talked about 'holding on'. What really caught my attention was when the writer talked about hanging on to the Word. So many times when we are going through things, we are told to just 'hold on', but hold on to what exactly? Hold on to your faith? Of course, but even your faith can wane. Hold on to God? Well, yes, because without Him you can do nothing, but it goes beyond than that. We need to hold on to His Word, which is forever settled.

When the devil tempted Jesus in the wilderness, he was attacking Jesus's very identity and trying to get Him to doubt who He was, but Jesus refused to give into the temptation. To every temptation the devil brought His way, Jesus responded, 'It is written'. You need to know what is written about you; not what people say or have said but what God says. It is written that you are the 'apple of God's eye' (Ps. 17:8, NKJV). It is written that 'you are more than a conqueror through Christ who loved you' (Rom. 8:37, NKJV, paraphrased). It is written that 'you are fearfully and wonderfully made' (Ps. 139:14, NKJV). I could go on and list all that the Bible says you are, but time and space will not permit me.

Our past experiences (if viewed from a proper perspective) contribute to the great people we eventually become, but they should not define us nor become our identity. What do I mean? The fact that you don't have a job right now and haven't had one for the last year does not mean that you are unemployable. Or just because you made some bad decisions in the past does not mean that you are incapable of making right choices. You are not your past or your experiences; you are the righteousness of God in Christ Jesus. The Bible says, 'This means that anyone who belongs to Christ has become a new person. The old life is gone; a new life has begun!' (2 Cor. 5:17, NLT)

When your situation and circumstances begin to talk to you, you have to know who you are in Christ and talk back. You have to know what God's Word says about the matter at hand, and it is that Word that you hold on to when things are difficult. You cling to the truth and unwavering power of God's Word until you see that truth come to pass in your life. You are not defeated because of what you are going through, but rather your defeat occurs when you give up and stop believing. So when life throws you lemons, grab hold of the Word and make lemonade, for this too shall pass.

The Battle Is Not Yours!

Exodus 3:7-8, New Living Translation

Then the Lord told him, 'I have certainly seen the oppression of my people in Egypt. I have heard their cries of distress because of their harsh slave drivers. Yes, I am aware of their suffering.[8] So I have come down to rescue them from the power of the Egyptians and lead them out of Egypt into their own fertile and spacious land. It is a land flowing with milk and honey . . .'

God is not unaware of where you are or what you are going through. God is not asleep! His Word says that He has seen your affliction, He understands your pain and He is full of compassion. 'For we do not have a High Priest Who is unable to understand and sympathise and have a shared feeling with our weaknesses and infirmities and liability to the assaults of temptation, but One Who has been tempted in every respect as we are, yet without sinning' (Heb. 4:15, AMP).

Notice what the Lord says, 'I have come down to bring you out and bring you up'. God will meet you where you are, wherever that maybe and rest assured that when He does, it will be to bring you into more than your mind could ever have conceived. When God takes you from one level to the next, it is always to a place that is prosperous and favourable (a place flowing with milk and honey). That is not to say that there won't be challenges along the way, but even in the midst of the trials, He is with you. We've all heard the phrase, 'No pain, no gain', which is used when referring to worldly things that come at a price, such as trying to lose weight, training for a marathon, ballet classes and so on. If by secular standards, we know that anything worth having involves some sort of pain and/or sacrifice, why do we expect any different when it comes to the things of God?

God wasn't oblivious to the struggles of the Israelites even though they thought He was. He categorically told the children of Israel that He would deliver them out of the hands of their oppressors and take them into a bountiful land. Sometimes we get frustrated and angry with God when He doesn't act immediately on an issue, and then we try to take matters into our own hands, but some battles in life are not ours to fight. God is very aware of what is going on and He has everything under control. 'The Lord is your Protector and He won't go to sleep or let you stumble' (Ps. 121:3, CEV).

The journey to the Promised Land is always fraught with trials and temptations, but the enemy has already been defeated and you win!

You Shall Not Be Moved!

Psalm 125:1-2, New Living Translation

Those who trust in the Lord are as secure as Mount Zion; they will not be defeated but will endure forever. Just as the mountains surround Jerusalem, so the Lord surrounds his people, both now and forever.

The Bible likens those who trust in God to Mount Zion, in that they cannot be moved. Some dictionary definitions of secure are free from or not exposed to danger or harm; safe; not liable to fail; safe from penetration or interception by unauthorised persons. In other words, if you trust in God, you are shielded and cannot lose. Therefore by extension, trusting in anything other than God leaves you vulnerable to attack with no protection.

When you put your trust in the world's system, you are exposed to the same consequences as those in the world. When you trust in the world's financial system rather than God as your source, you are subject to the frailties of that system. This is evidenced by the current economic climate, where many people put their trust and faith in houses, jobs, stock markets, shares and so on. When the recession hit, many of these people lost their homes, their jobs, and saw the value of their investments tumble. All of a sudden, institutions that people had trusted in for years collapsed before their very eyes. Age-old financial systems did what no one expected; they crumbled.

If you were to gamble, you wouldn't bet on something unstable or uncertain, would you? You would put your money on something that has the greatest probability of winning based on a number of factors, such as previous history, experience, skill and so on, but there is nothing guaranteed in this life. Everything is subject to change. However, the good news is that there is someone who does not change—He is the 'same yesterday, today and forever' (Heb. 13:8, NLT). He is not one thing today and something completely different tomorrow. In a world of constant change, there is one that remains constant; His name is Jesus.

Put you trust in Jesus! When you do, you will never be defeated by life's challenges. No matter what comes your way, you will stand tall, immoveable, and unshakeable like Mount Zion. When you put your trust in Him, He will surround you like the mountains surround Jerusalem and form a hedge of protection around you. This is a wonderful picture—anything or anyone trying to get to you will have to go through God first! When you put your trust in Him, you shall not be moved.

The Testing of Your Faith

James 1:2-4, New Living Translation

Dear brothers and sisters when troubles come your way, consider it an opportunity for great joy. For you know that when your faith is tested, your endurance has a chance to grow. So let it grow for when your endurance is fully developed, you will be perfect and complete, needing nothing.

The story of Lazarus teaches us that God is not ignorant of the things we go through nor does He lack compassion. When Jesus learnt of Lazarus's sickness, He waited a further two days before going to see him. Why? Not because Jesus didn't care or because He wanted Mary and Martha to suffer, but rather so that the glory and power of God would be evident to the people. Having been dead for four days, Lazarus's body would have started to decay and smell, so there would be no doubt in anyone's mind that Jesus raised Lazarus from the dead.

Sometimes God will permit or use (not create!) difficult circumstances in your life to test your faith in Him and His Word. It is under pressure that the condition of your heart is revealed. What do you really believe? Does what is in your heart line up with the words coming out of your mouth? When your faith is put to the test, do you hold fast to your confession or do you begin to complain and question God?

In times of trouble, we are to remain committed to the Word and recognise that God is the one ordering our steps. Nothing takes God by surprise; He is never unprepared and neither should you be. He went ahead of you to prepare the way and left you His Word to guide you, so that nothing would take you by surprise. When troubles come your way, the psalmist instructs you to lift up your eyes to the hills—'I will lift up my eyes to the hills—From whence comes my help? My help comes from the LORD, Who made heaven and earth' (Ps. 121:1-2, NKJV). When sickness comes knocking at the door, Jesus said, '. . . by His cuts and bruises you are healed' (1 Pet. 2:24, CEV). It's not all doom and gloom, for it is those difficult times that glorious testimonies are born. It is in the midst of the problems that you see the faithfulness and grace of God at work.

Let me share with you an analogy used by my pastor to explain problems. He said problems are like exams, which are in effect tests. Exams or tests do not come to make you more intelligent, but rather to find out how intelligent you are. Exams are designed to test what you know, and when you sit the exam, the examiner is silent. There is a saying that what doesn't kill you, only makes you stronger! This is in effect what James is saying. Some tests you pass, some you fail, but with each test, your knowledge of what to expect grows and so does your level of maturity. You need to begin to see problems as pathways to progress, pit stops to the palace and prerequisites for promotion. Be encouraged; it's just a test!

God's Armour

Ephesians 6:11-13, 16, New Living Translation

Put on all of God's armour so that you will be able to stand firm against all strategies of the devil; for we are not fighting against flesh-and-blood enemies, but against evil rulers and authorities of the unseen world, against mighty powers in this dark world, and against evil spirits in the heavenly places. Therefore, put on every piece of God's armour so you will be able to resist the enemy in the time of evil. Then after the battle you will still be standing firm . . . In addition to all of these, hold up the shield of faith to stop the fiery arrows of the devil.

The Bible tells us that we are in a spiritual battle, meaning that a lot of the physical things we see are as a result of things happening in the spiritual realm. Therefore to fight effectively, our weapons need to be spiritual. Every battle has to be approached with the appropriate armoury or weaponry. You wouldn't go to war with a bow and arrow when your enemies were in possession of hand grenades and rifles. As silly as this may sound, this is what we do. Oftentimes, we try and approach spiritual problems with physical solutions.

In the book of Ephesians, we are instructed to put on God's complete armour in order to withstand the temptations and schemes of the devil. Picture a warrior in ancient times dressed and ready for battle. His body is sheathed in protective clothing, in one hand a spear or sword, and in the other hand a shield to protect him against the weapons fired by the enemy. It's the same for us as Christians. We are told to put on the breastplate of righteousness, take up our sword, which is the Word of God and carry our shield of faith, but what does this mean in real terms?

A breastplate is a piece of armour worn over the torso to protect it from injury; it protects the vital organs without limiting movement. By virtue of your faith in Jesus Christ, 'You are the righteousness of God in Christ Jesus' (2 Cor. 5:21, NKJV) and therefore when you put on the breastplate of righteousness, you put on Christ. So when the enemy tries to bring condemnation upon you because of your past or mistakes you have made, Jesus intercedes for you with the Father. So when the Father sees you, He sees Christ! When the enemy attacks you with troubles, you fight back with the sword of the spirit and proclaim the Word of God over that situation 'For the word of God is living and powerful, and sharper than any two-edged sword, piercing even to the division of soul and spirit, and of joints and marrow . . .' (Heb. 4:12, NKJV). When the enemy comes against you with feelings of inadequacy, you lift up your shield of faith as a defence to protect you.

As Christians, we are instructed to 'Stay alert! Watch out for your great enemy, the devil. He prowls around like a roaring lion, looking for someone to devour' (1 Pet. 5:8, NLT). Therefore, be on your guard always and before you go to war with the enemy, make sure you are dressed for battle!

When You're Feeling Discouraged . . .

'Do not be afraid or discouraged, for the Lord will personally go ahead of you. He will be with you; he will neither fail you nor abandon you.' (Deut. 31:8)

Just Keep Standing!

1 Corinthians 15:58, New Century Version

So my dear brothers and sisters, stand strong. Do not let anything move you.

What do you do when you feel like giving up? What do you do when things don't appear to be changing? When it feels like your life is one step forward and two steps backwards? The Bible says, 'When you've done all you know to do, you stand!'

Our biggest challenge as people is consistency and continuity. By this, I mean seeing things through to the end and remaining steadfast until what we are waiting for comes to pass. The only way to test the strength or durability of a material is to increase the pressure and/or temperature applied to the material and to observe what happens. Take a rubber band for example. If you apply a little pressure and it snaps, then of what use is it to you? The further you can stretch it without it giving way, the more durable it is. In relationships, if your first instinct is to run or give up when problems arise, then you are not ready for a committed relationship. If lack of money is your problem, God can't bless you with more money until you have shown that you can handle the little you have. Do you give to others that are in need? Are you paying off what you owe or continually spending on credit? Sometimes it's not about your staying power; it's about your character. What do you do when the pressure is on? How do you respond when the heat is turned up?

Pressure on the outside eventually reveals what's on the inside. Gold starts of as a metallic yellow substance and then it goes through a refining process, where it is heated to very high temperatures to remove all traces of impurity. The end product is the beautiful jewellery we see in stores like Ernest Jones and Tiffany's; however, it's important to remember—that's not how the product starts off.

Many times we get so consumed with a picture of how our lives should be or where we are going that we end up discouraged when things don't go according to plan. Inasmuch as you have your plans, God has a master plan. The book of Proverbs says, 'We can make our plans but the Lord determines our steps' (Prov. 16:9, NLT). Yes, you've heard this all before, but that doesn't make it any less true.

Life is a refining pot of experiences—some pleasant and some less, but with one thing in common: they are all fitting into God's perfect plan for your life. So when you've done all you know to do, continue to stand firmly on God's Word. Everything else around you may fail, but His Word never fails!

The Seasons of Life

Genesis 8:22, New Living Translation

As long as the earth remains, there will be planting and harvest, cold and heat, summer and winter, day and night.

Life is comprised of seasons. The dictionary definition of 'season'[3] is 'one of the four periods of the year (spring, summer, autumn, and winter). It is a period of the year characterised by particular conditions of weather, temperature and so on'. Spring is a time when trees bud, plants grow and the weather becomes warmer. Summer is 'the period of finest development, perfection or beauty'. Autumn is 'a time of full maturity', and winter is the 'period of decline, decay, inertia, dreariness, or adversity'.

When we go through difficult times, we get angry with God, thinking He has abandoned us or we blame the devil and failing that, some ancient family curse or the fact that things just never work for us. God is in control of your life, so before you pack away your Bible and turn your back on God, take an objective look at things and prayerfully try to understand what season you are in.

Let me help you put Genesis 8:22 into perspective. It means that as long as the earth continues to revolve around its axis and you continue to live in this world, there will be times in your life when you will experience lack and abundance, sowing and reaping, adversity and favour. God uses the difficult seasons in your life to deal with your character—Are you a man (or woman) of your word? What do you do when things don't go your way? Do you throw a temper tantrum or do you take it to God in prayer? Can you be trusted with money? Do you shout first and ask questions later? God is more interested in refining your character than making you comfortable! Your tears don't move God; they fill Him with compassion, but they do not sway Him from His purpose, which is that all men should be saved. You are His living epistle in a world of immorality, darkness and depravity.

You may be in that season of growth, where after months, or possibly years of hardship, you are now seeing the budding fruits of your labour. For others, you are in the autumn season of life, a period of maturity, which is never comfortable. It often means dying to old habits, learning to wait patiently for answered prayer in certain areas, whereas previously in other areas the answer was swift and immediate. Sometimes we see people, who have what we desire and we envy them, but we don't know what they went through to get what they have now. You see them basking in their summer season, but you have no idea what they went through in the winter season of their life.

We will always have seasons in our lives—seasons of spring and summer and autumn and winter—it's called the cycle of life. While the spiritual seasons in our life do not always have the same time span as the natural seasons, we are assured in God's Word that our times and seasons are in His hands. Seasons may come and go, but God remains God in all seasons!

You Are Not Alone

Isaiah 43:2, New Living Translation

When you go through deep waters, I will be with you. When you go through rivers of difficulty, you will not drown. When you walk through the fire of oppression, you will not be burned up; the flames will not consume you.

Jesus knew that there would be times when you will feel discouraged, that's why He left you His Word. His promise to you is that the trials will not overwhelm you, neither will they consume or overtake you.

In the above scripture, notice that there is 'a going through'. You can't escape or avoid challenges, but the good news is that each challenge is followed by the promise of victory. This is in line with John 16:33, NLT, where Jesus says, 'I have told you all this so that you may have peace in Me. Here on earth you will have many trials and sorrows, but take heart, because I have overcome the world.' God did not promise you a trouble-free life, but He promised you victory because He has overcome the world.

There is something Joyce Meyer said that resonated within me and got me thinking in a new way. She said, 'Jesus went through some things so you wouldn't have to and other things to show you how to get through.' This quote by Joyce Meyer provides much needed perspective because oftentimes, when we go through struggles, we develop a woe-is-me kind of attitude and question why certain things are happening. In some instances, we become angry with God. After all, He should have prevented the problem, but you cannot escape life. As long as you live and breathe, your life will never be devoid of challenges. We live in a fallen world, and every day we see the effects of sin and man's refusal to accept God.

There are some things you will just have to go through, but the guarantee you have is that whatever the situation, God is with you and He will not allow you to go through more than you can bear.' The temptations in your life are no different from what others experience. And God is faithful. He will not allow the temptation to be more than you can stand. When you are tempted, He will show you a way out so that you can endure' (1 Cor. 10:13, NLT). That is why you survived what destroyed others. In your darkest and loneliest moments, though it may not feel like it, rest assured God is very much with you, for He promised never to leave you nor forsake you.

Not Easily Broken

2 Corinthians 4:8-9, The Living Bible

We are pressed on every side by troubles, but not crushed and broken. We are perplexed because we don't know why things happen as they do but we don't give up and quit. We are hunted down but God never abandons us. We get knocked down but we get up again and keep going.

I love this particular scripture because it speaks of survival; it speaks of help! For many of us these two verses are a picture of what life has been like in the past couple of months or past year, for some even the last few years—struggle after struggle, challenge after challenge, and one trouble after the next. It seems like you have spent more time 'fire fighting' than anything else. Every which way you turn there is another situation to be conquered, another process to walk through and another stepping-stone to a testimony.

You may feel like there is nowhere to go and no one for you to turn to, but there is hope. You shall come out of your current situation. There is no situation beyond God's control, no person beyond redemption and no temptation that cannot be overcome. In whatever predicament you find yourself, know that you are not alone. The above scripture is an extract from Paul's letter to the church in Corinth, where he talks about the price followers of Christ pay for serving Him. As it was in Paul's day, so it is today. We face all manner of tests and trials, but we are not destroyed in the process. Sometimes the pressure of what you are going through is so intense that you truly believe that you won't make it through, yet you do. The sun goes down at night and you live to see it rise in the morning. Why? Because God is with you! You've heard it said that the presence of problems does not indicate the absence of God. This is not a cliché to be thrown about when things get tough; this is true. Even in your 'bad' days, God is with you. Jesus said, '. . . And be sure of this: I am with you always, even to the end of the age' (Matt. 28:20, NLT). He remains faithful even when you are faithless! That is why you may get shaken up and in some cases, even knocked down, but you are able to get up and keep going.

Everything you have been through is fitting into God's divine plan and will ultimately work out in your favour. Romans 8:28, MSG, tells us, 'That's why we can be so sure that every detail in our lives of love for God is worked into something good.' You will look back on the hard times and give thanks to God who sustained you through each dark day and brought you out in joy. For everything you have lost, the Lord shall restore unto you. When you've reached the end of yourself, you've reached the beginning of God!

He Is Your Rock

Psalm 40:2-3, New Living Translation

He lifted me out of the pit of despair, out of the mud and the mire. He set my feet on solid ground and steadied me as I walked along. He has given me a new song to sing, a hymn of praise to our God. Many will see what he has done and be amazed. They will put their trust in the Lord.

I'm going to ask the question, even though I know most people will say, 'Are you for real?' Have you ever felt so discouraged that you just don't know what to do with yourself? I've gone through periods in my life where I have felt, what's the point of it all? Praying had become a chore and going to church an inconvenience, but the thing is when you have the spirit of God in you, He just won't leave you alone. Something within you will drive you to your knees in prayer, even though your mouth refuses to cooperate. Your eyes scan the pages of scripture and even though the words don't seem to register, something deep within you comes alive; hope is reignited. You suddenly think perhaps there is a chance that this is not how the story ends; perhaps this light affliction really is temporary; perhaps that proverbial silver lining on the edge of the cloud is getting bigger.

The Word of God really is life to your bones. When the Word of God is spoken over a situation, suddenly things don't seem as bad as they first appeared. In fact, things could be so much worse. I was reading a particular copy of the *Word for Today*, and it told the story of a quadriplegic and all the great things she had gone on to do despite her obvious limitations. When you think about it, the reasons we give ourselves for not doing things are really just excuses. The dictionary definition of an excuse is 'to free, as from an obligation or duty'. Excuses are a crutch; they are our everyday 'get out clause!'

There is no situation that is bigger than God! Your life could have been over, but somehow you are here, alive to live another day. People including loved ones wrote you off, but they didn't count on the unconditional love of a God who reaches out to you even in times of doubt and despair. Your life is already a testimony of who God is and what He has done. Discouragement only arises when you stop believing God and start believing the lies of the enemy.

God is faithful even when you are not. 'If we are faithless, He remains faithful for He cannot deny who He is' (2 Tim. 2:13, NLT). God will never leave you alone; He is with you always. When you reach the point of giving up, speak the words from 2 Chronicles 20:12 (AMP), '. . . We do not know what to do, but our eyes are upon You'.

The Sovereignty of God . . .

'I am the Alpha and the Omega, the First and
the Last, the Beginning and the End.
(Rev. 22:13)

Who Is Like God?

Job 38:1-11, 19-21, New Living Translation

Then the Lord answered Job from the whirlwind:

Who is this that questions my wisdom with such ignorant words?
Brace yourself like a man because I have some questions for you and you must
answer them. 'Where were you when I laid the foundations of the earth? Tell me, if
you know so much. Who determined its dimensions and stretched out the surveying
line? What supports its foundations, and who laid its cornerstone as the morning
stars sang together and all the angels shouted for joy? Who kept the sea inside its
boundaries as it burst from the womb, and as I clothed it with clouds and wrapped
it in thick darkness? For I locked it behind barred gates, limiting its shores. I said,
'This far and no farther will you come. Here your proud waves must stop!' Where
does light come from, and where does darkness go? Can you take each to its home?
Do you know how to get there? But of course you know all this! For you were born
before it was all created, and you are so very experienced!

Those who question the existence of God have proposed a theory that our existence is as a result of apes evolving into humans. They argue that everything exists as a result of random events and by virtue of a big collision of atoms or what is commonly known as the 'Big Bang!' However, when you ponder on creation and observe the order of things, the idea that everything came into being randomly yet so perfectly is more absurd than believing that God created the universe.

When I read this conversation between God and Job, I was chastised and at the same time humbled by the awesomeness of God. Really, who am I to question God? When I've mastered the art of creation and created my first human being from scratch then perhaps I might be able to send in a few questions to the 'I *Am* that I *Am*!' Until then, it's probably wise to keep my questions to myself. Now, don't get me wrong. I'm not saying we should never ask questions of God. Sometimes if your life is stagnant and there is no evidence of progress or you keep meeting the same problem time and time again, then in such times I would say it is prudent to check in with God as perhaps there is something you need to deal with. Maybe you haven't obeyed His last instruction, or dare I say it, perhaps there is sin in the camp.

It's very easy to question whether God actually knows what He's doing or whether He's just playing Russian roulette with our lives, but when you look at the beauty of the universe, you have to know that God might just have an idea or two! He is the Creator of all things, yet He himself is not created. He is 'El Elyon'—the Most High God. He is not bound by time or space, yet He is in all places at all times, and in all times, in all seasons. To question God is to question your very existence! When you find yourself questioning God, look around you. Everything you see is proof that God is Sovereign. He is in full control of your life and nothing happens by chance!

God of Heaven and Earth

Deuteronomy 4:34-39, New Living Translation

Has any other god dared to take a nation for himself out of another nation by means of trials, miraculous signs, wonders, war, a strong hand, a powerful arm, and terrifying acts? Yet that is what the Lord your God did for you in Egypt, right before your eyes. He showed you these things so you would know that the Lord is God and there is no other. He let you hear his voice from heaven so he could instruct you. He let you see his great fire here on earth so he could speak to you from it. Because he loved your ancestors, he chose to bless their descendants, and he personally brought you out of Egypt with a great display of power. He drove out nations far greater than you, so he could bring you in and give you their land as your special possession, as it is today. 'So remember this and keep it firmly in mind: The Lord is God both in heaven and on earth, and there is no other'.

While reading this scripture, I was blown away by the visible display of love shown by an invisible God. The scripture talks about God delivering the Israelites out of Egypt, a story we've heard so many times and could probably recite in our sleep. However, while reading this story one day, I saw something I had never really seen before, or at least had never fully appreciated! The lengths God went to for a people who ignored Him time and time again; the people who saw daily evidence of His omnipotence and omniscience yet still they would complain and murmur and doubt; kind of what we do today.

The Bible is the Word of God written not just for our admonishment, neither is it written to entertain, but rather to give us a picture of who God is and encourage us in our times of struggle. The Bible is littered with stories of people no different from you and me who faced the same battles, the same weaknesses, and yet they remained steadfast in the Lord.

In this scripture, Moses is calling to the remembrance of the people the things God had delivered them from. Why? So that when they entered the Promised Land, they would not forget all that God had done because certainly they would face further challenges. If God could deliver the Israelites time and time again, how much more us who are children of a New Covenant? He is God, and there is no other! He created the heavens and the earth by the words of His mouth. Psalm 33:6, NKJV, says, 'By the word of the Lord the heavens were made and all the host of them by the breath of His mouth.'

The prophet Jeremiah understood the greatness of God. He said, 'Ah, Lord GOD! Behold, You have made the heavens and the earth by Your great power and outstretched arm. There is nothing too hard for You' (Jer. 32:17, NKJV). People will fight against you and contend with you, but they shall not prevail for the Lord is with you. You need to stop talking about the magnitude of the problem and boast about the greatness of your God!

God Is Still God!

Hebrews 13:8, New Living Translation

Jesus Christ is the same yesterday, today, and forever.

World economies are being shaken; job losses are in the thousands and long-established financial institutions are crumbling before our very eyes. Sickness is seeping its way through families, wreaking havoc and despair; civil wars are tearing nations apart . . . *yet* in the midst of it all, God remains God!

As a human being, the tendency is to panic at the chaos, *but* in the midst of all this change and uncertainty, there is a God that does not change! If your trust is in God, if your reliance is on Him, then you too shall not be moved by what is happening around you.

I once read in a devotional something that is so apt for the times we are in now, yet it was written many, many years ago. The author Kenneth E. Hagin said and I quote, 'Whenever God knocks the props from beneath our feet it is in order that we might rest more securely on Him'. He also said that, 'God is allowing kingdoms to be shaken so that they might discover the unshakeable kingdom—the Kingdom of God!'

This season we find ourselves in has been termed the 'credit crunch', and perhaps it is a pertinent title. After all, the credit of anything (person or establishment) is only as good as the value or trust you place in that thing. Perhaps God is 'crunching' all those systems that men have come to depend upon and elevated above God? This is the time to search deep within and identify what you have made your security blanket? What have you been trusting in? Is it the housing market or the stock market? Or maybe it's your job or even your qualifications? God doesn't need any of these things to achieve His purpose.

Nothing in this world is certain or guaranteed; everything is subject to change, *but* there is One on whom you can depend, the One who is reaching out to you in the midst of the turmoil and distress and saying, 'Be still and know that I am God' (Ps. 46:10, NKJV). You may not know what tomorrow may bring; you may not even know what the next hour or day may bring, but one thing you can be sure of is that in all situations, God is still God! He says of Himself, 'I am the Lord All-Powerful, and I never change' (Mal. 3:6, CEV). He is still God in the good times and the bad times. Therefore, in this period of economic upheaval, put your hope in God. Your dependency on this unshakeable God will cause you to remain standing when everything around you is falling.

What Do You Know?

Psalm 46:10, New Living Translation

'Be still, and know that I am God . . .'

Even though the character and workings of God are preached from the pulpit, personal experience still is and will always remain the best teacher.

Sometimes the area of your greatest struggle is the area of your greatest blessing. I am gradually accepting in my head what my heart already knows, that I will never feel equipped or qualified for the things I am called to do. As I ponder on these things, I am taken aback at the enormity of the task, but at the same time, I am humbly encouraged!

It's not about the skills or abilities you possess or do not possess. It's not about your degree or lack thereof. None of that matters! God's purpose and plans will always prevail, whether it's through you or somebody else. The Bible declares that He has intentionally chosen the foolish things of this world, those who are weak and those from seemingly insignificant or troubled backgrounds to put to shame those who think they are wise and important (1 Cor. 1:27, NKJV, paraphrased). He has deliberately chosen you (yes, you!). In the eyes of the world, your weaknesses and background make you unsuitable, but God's ways are not the ways of the world, and the very things you lack or you think are holding you back make you a perfect candidate. Consider Moses, a man of anger used mightily by God to deliver the people of Israel. What about Simon Peter? He denied Christ three times, yet God used him mightily to start the early church? Should I mention Jacob, the deceiver who tricked his way into his brother's birthright but was the father of the twelve tribes of Israel? Time and space prevent me from naming the many great men and women, like you and me with human failings, who were used by God to accomplish great things. By the time God is through with you, those who have looked down at you in contempt, or ridiculed and criticised you will not be able to explain it. They will not be able to rationalise who you are with where you were. So stop trying to be perfect or feel qualified. The only thing God requires of you is that you have faith in Him.

Knowing God comes from a place of trust. Trust that His timing is perfect and that His plans for you are ultimately good. Stop questioning, doubting, and second-guessing yourself, but more importantly, stop procrastinating. One thing I'm learning is that faith is not just about saying what you believe, but also acting on what you know and believe to be true. So I ask you, what do you know?

I hope this collection of devotions blessed you. It is not intended to criticise, judge or condemn, but rather show that we are all work in progress and that the solution to every problem can be found in God and the infallibility of His Word.

When you are confused, it will bring clarity, for the Bible says 'Your word is a lamp to guide my feet and a light for my path' (Ps. 119:105). When you are upset, the Word of God will bring comfort, so 'weeping may endure for a night but joy cometh in the morning (Ps. 30:5).' When you need direction, God says in His Word, 'Call unto me and I will show you great and mighty things you did not know' (Jer. 33:3). When you are in need, the Bible tells us that 'Our God shall supply all our need according to His riches in glory' (Phil. 4:19).

Many of us are still waiting for God to do something. When asked what is preventing us from stepping out or making a move, our response is 'I am waiting on God'. The sad thing is, God is waiting on you. There is nothing left for God to do. He did all He needed to do when He sent His Son, Jesus, to pay the price for your sins on the cross of Calvary. He has given you authority and dominion over every situation through Jesus Christ. Life is not about our comfort; it's about being a blessing and a help to those around us. You were created for a reason; you are or hold the solution to a problem without which you will always feel discontented or unfulfilled.

Take control of the negative thoughts that try and weigh your down; respond to fear with boldness; attack doubt with faith and ignore people that say you will never make it or things will never get better. We need to stop living like victims and hold our heads high as the victors we are, for the battle has already been won. We are here to enjoy the spoils of that victory, but more importantly, share the news of this victory with others. A life dedicated to the service of self is no life at all!

Remain Blessed!

Glossary

Different translations of the Bible have been used in this book. The following abbreviations have been used to conserve space:

AMP—Amplified Bible
CEB—Common English Bible
CEV—Contemporary English Version
NKJV—The New King James Version
NLT—New Living Translation
MSG—The Message Translation

Endnotes

1   *www.speakfaith.com*
2   *A Heart of Devotion* by Tia McCollors.
3   *www.dictionary.com*